TRAINING SOCCER CHAMPIONS

BY ANSON DORRANCE
With Tim Nash

Training Soccer Champions

was published in the USA by
JTC Sports, Inc.
1207 Brittany Point Ct.
Apex, NC 27502
(919) 303-6611
Publisher: Janice T. Cheves

Design by Shari Sasser, Sasser Studios
Cover Photo by J. Brett Whitesell, R&B Sports Photography
Back Cover Photo by Mike Stahlschmidt, Sideline Sports Photography
Additional photos: Page 18, Anson Dorrance by Andrew Cline; Page 44, Carla
Overbeck by Mike Stahlschmidt; Page 62, NCAA celebration by David Minton; Page
90, Kristin Acquavella (8), Mia Hamm (center) and Angie Kelly frame the goal by J.
Brett Whitesell; Page 102, Carolina Goal by Andrew Cline

Editorial Assistance provided by Harold Nash, M'Liss Dorrance, Steve Kirschner,
Tom Sander, Steve Payne, Delaine Marbry

Computer match analysis provided by Softsport,
P.O. Box 4967 West Hills, CA 91308-4967
Peer Evaluation provided by Peer Plus, Inc.
113 Carolina Ave., Chapel Hill, NC 27514

ISBN 1-887791-02-7

Printed in the United States of America

Table of Contents

Dedication

I would like to dedicate this book
to my gentleman coach, Dr. Marvin Allen.
He made it honorable for all those who followed him
and made everything possible for me.

Acknowledgments

I just got off the phone with April Heinrichs. She was calling from Brazil as the assistant coach for Tony DiCicco and the U.S. Women's National Team. I told her how much I enjoyed training her when she was a fantastic right wing for me at the University of North Carolina. I told her how lucky I have been to work with so many amazing athletes over the years.

"Training Soccer Champions", the title Tim Nash selected for this book, is a very appropriate description of what I've had the opportunity to do since I was given my first women's team in 1979. I have always felt I was given champions, and it was my job to somehow give them an opportunity to showcase their level of talent and desire. It is unfortunate that this book does not give me enough space to credit all of the amazing young women who have taught me so much about this game and how to relate to the people who play it. There is no formula or alchemy for a champion. It always begins with the player — the size of their heart, their work ethic and their willingness to take physical risks. I have always been fortunate to have these people play for me at North Carolina and for the United States Women's National Team.

Little of what we have at North Carolina has been developed or designed without Bill Palladino, my good friend. And I am sure that the parts of the program which were developed without him are the parts that aren't fun. His impact is so significant, I could not tell you where I end and where he begins. While I am on the subject of crucial people, I would like to set the record straight about the 1991 World Championship — the only significant tactical decision during that championship was made by Laurie Gregg. Her work ethic and raw intelligence were the foundation of our assault on the international game, and I have always wanted a public forum to share that.

When I was a young soccer coach, I used to hide behind the pedigree of my foreign upbringing. I was born in Bombay, India, and at the age of two my family moved to Calcutta. Every three years or so we moved, going next to Nairobi, Kenya, then to Addis Ababa, Ethiopia. Then, after a short stint in Oakland, California, we moved to Singapore, Malaysia. My family then had short stops in Louisburg, North Carolina, and White Plains, New York, before we moved to Brussels, Belgium. While my family was in Brussels, I was sent to a boys' boarding school in Fribourg, Switzerland, for my high school education. It was not until I came to college — one semester at St. Mary's in San Antonio, Texas, and the next four-and-a-half years at the University of North Carolina — that I spent any signifi-

8

cant time in the United States. When I was young and insecure, this litany of foreign countries would lend credibility to what I thought was a lackluster soccer resumé. In reality, as an American raised abroad I became a fervent patriot. And out of a chauvinistic desire to be more American, I played American sports in my free time as much as possible, sports like touch football, basketball and softball. Even when those opportunities were not available, like when we lived in Kenya, I played field hockey and rugby like all the young British imperialists I was being educated with at the time.

In April of 1991, I had a remarkable experience in Haiti at a press conference following an explosive performance by our women's national team. We had just qualified for the first FIFA Women's World Championships by out-scoring our five opponents 49-0. I was fielding questions about our wonderful team. This was a very soccer-educated press corps, and they were trying to get to the core reason why we were so attractive to watch. Where are your players from? What do you do in training? How long have you been together? How many of your players have been developed in foreign leagues or raised abroad? None of my answers satisfied them until one of them asked, "What's your background?" I told them about all the different countries I had lived in, and they all nodded knowingly. They concluded that I had learned my soccer abroad, and this influence had impacted on what they could not believe was an American team. But for the first time, I had the confidence to tell the truth: I learned how to play soccer at the University of North Carolina-Chapel Hill ... I learned how to coach soccer at the United States Soccer Federation coaching schools and from the clinics at the National Soccer Coaches Association of America annual convention ... and all our players had been developed in American leagues with American coaches.

Seven months later, after we had won the World Championship, I concluded each speech by telling everyone that I was proud to be an American, proud to be a product of our coaching system and proud to be a world champion. I was very proud to tell everyone that it has never been our coaches and players that could not compete at the highest level. It was our environment that was lacking. We did not have an elite league in place long enough to impact on the indefatigable American spirit and allow us to showcase our true potential. In the women's game, at last we had it. The high levels of American Division I collegiate programs, the excellent youth Olympic Development system and select club programs at that time were as good as those in any of the foreign countries we were competing against. Our wonderful player development system leveled the international playing field for us for the first time. The receptions following that championship were swelling with the same pride I had, vindicating what all of us felt: The U.S. could organize a team at any level — male or female — to compete with the best. We had the administrative infrastructure. We had the coaches, and we had the players. We just needed the competitive environment to nurture them.

My personal debts to the many people who helped me will never be repaid, but let me at least thank them. My own college coach, Dr. Marvin Allen, the 1969 Honor Award Winner, had the grace to recommend me to Bill Cobey, the UNC athletic director who hired me as an unproven twenty-four-year-old in 1976. And Mr. Cobey had the wisdom in 1979 to begin a varsity women's soccer program in Chapel Hill when there was no other in the South. Moyer Smith, the president of the Educational Foundation, made sure scholarship money would not be an issue, and John Swofford, the current athletic director at UNC, aggressively supported us to be competitive nationally. I appreciate the weekly guidance from our associate athletic director, Dick Baddour, and the daily consternation Beth Miller, my immediate supervisor, must go through as she tries to administrate my free spirit. Great thanks to John Lotz, my personal motivator for his gentle and constant positive presence.

My soccer influences are many and varied, but let me begin with Dr. Tom Fleck, who had confidence in me before he should have, and Walt Chyzowych, Art Walls and Jim Rudy, who gave me my first chances. Back then, in the late-seventies and early-eighties, my mentors were a collage. I wanted to be able to speak like Cliff McCrath, organize myself like Joe Morrone, have the tactical understanding of Jim Lennox and Jay Miller, the presence of Bob Gansler and the class of Bill Schellenberger. Although I did not succeed in any category, I always wanted to aspire to a high standard. I hope some of the things I have shared in this book convey that ambition.

Forward
By Tim Nash

Through a fluke of geography, I got to know Anson Dorrance. When I moved to North Carolina in 1987, I lived 20 minutes from Chapel Hill, and fortunately for me, my first view of a big-time women's college soccer game came when I watched the University of North Carolina systematically dismantle Maryland in the first-ever Atlantic Coast Conference Tournament. I was very, very impressed.

As I walked to my seat, Carolina scored. Then Maryland kicked off, and I mean kicked off. One player touched it to another and boom. I almost walked back out when I saw that the Terrapins didn't bother crossing the halfway line. Soon I realized that Maryland knew it was pointless. After the kickoff, Carolina gathered the ball, moved quickly up the field, put the ball into the corner, and hit a cross. Another Carolina player picked the ball out of the air, back-heeling it to a teammate at the eighteen-yard line. The UNC player hit a one-touch rocket just under the crossbar. Needless to say, I stayed. I soon learned about the streaks and the incredible, almost laughable, record UNC had compiled over the years. I became fascinated with the program. I went to UNC games with the same morbid curiosity that people have when they slow down to see a car accident. I felt if I didn't go, I might miss something. I would go for one half, ten minutes, or I would just stop by after watching another game in the area. In 1988, I started covering soccer in the ACC area, and I interviewed Anson on many occasions. There are very few questions reporters can ask a coach who wins all the time that he hasn't heard before. But with each conversation, I learned bits and pieces. I became more and more curious as to how this program sustained such an incredible winning streak.

One day seven years after I first saw Carolina play, Anson was outside the main gate at UNC's Fetzer Field with his wife, who evidently had just gone home to get the tie Anson had forgotten. I lurked nearby. Anson took the tie and headed down the driveway to the Soccer Hut, an odd little structure outside of Fetzer Field that serves as a teamroom, storeroom, offices for the men's and women's soccer coaches and storage place for Anson's roller hockey sticks. I thought this was as good a time as any to approach him about an idea I had been kicking around.

"Anson!" I yelled. He stopped and said hello. Knowing that he certainly had a lot on his mind, the least of which was me or his tie, I jumped right into it.

"Wanna write a book?" I said.

"Sure," he said. "Write me up something."

"Okay," I said, and that was it.

A month later, I caught up to him again. This time we were in Houston at the Chevron/adidas Women's Soccer Challenge. His team had just beaten Vanderbilt, and he was settling in to watch Stanford play Duke. I handed him an envelope which contained an outline of a book called "Training Soccer Champions." He loved the idea, but warned me that I would have to hound him constantly to get it done. The next time we talked about the book was immediately following the press conference at the 1994 national finals in Portland, where his team won their thirteenth national title by beating Notre Dame 5-0. I set up the first interview for the book. A few weeks later, I went to Anson's office for the first interview. I had been in his office many times before, but I'm always amazed. His portion of The Hut is a little smaller than the six-yard box on a soccer field. It includes two filing cabinets, a small desk, a couch which doubles as a magazine rack, coffee table, book shelf, dresser drawer, and I think there's a chair in there somewhere underneath a couple of Hermann Trophies and some magazines. Looking around, it becomes obvious that at one time he had made an effort to display all the trophies, awards and photos he acquired over the years. He soon ran out of room. My first interview started badly, but quickly turned around. I had an outline, and I thought I would try to get him to stick to it. After the first day, I never referred to it again.

"Let's start with your basic coaching philosophy," I said. Well, I discovered that asking that question was like saying to someone, "Let's begin with your life story and then work from there." Anson had a much better idea: "Just get me started on something," he said. His way was more fun. From then on, it went very smoothly. I got to his office in the morning, brought up a topic and off he went. The following chapters consist of our conversations. His opinions are based on what his experiences over the years have told him are facts. Some are controversial. Some are revolutionary. What I found to be fascinating is that he has taken very basic aspects of soccer and found innovative and interesting ways to teach them to his players. And it works.

At the University of North Carolina, there are some simple reasons for the incredible success of the program. One is that players get better ... everyday. The great players get greater. The good players become great, and the average players become above average. The worst players get better and have a good time. A very important aspect of the UNC program is competition. As you will read, the competitive cauldron is what makes his players better. Based on the simple concept that the climate for developing players is better when competition exists, the cauldron arranges for players to be constantly challenged. But when the competition ends, so does the competitive atmosphere. I'll admit, I did not believe that the women in the UNC program could enjoy this type of atmosphere. I did not think they could bang each other around in practice and be best friends five minutes later. I was wrong.

During the interview process, Anson kept telling me to interview some of the players, and I always responded with, "Who would be a good one for me to talk to?" I assumed that, as with any team, there would be ones who would say nice things about him and the program and others who would trash his methods and philosophies. I wanted to avoid those people. But he kept telling me it didn't matter who I talked to, and I don't think he knew why I was asking. So I just started talking to players. And guess what? It's true. I also was able to draw some conclusions about Anson's personality. His mind is as organized as his office is disorganized. He is an intense competitor, who hates to lose. But he realizes that he is a coach, not a brain surgeon. He is keenly aware that he is not holding the key to life in his hands. As he said on many occasions, "It's just soccer." Anson also has a very high level of understanding about female athletes and what coaches can do to ensure maximum performance from their players. I believe there are very few aspects of coaching that don't interest Anson. There are soccer coaches whose styles are based in science — formations, formulas, human mechanics and equations all play a part in their team's system. And there are coaches whose styles are based on art — expressions of freedom, personal creativity of the players, and imagination. Anson has a unique mix of both. We had conversations ranging from European and Scandinavian cultures and how they affect women's soccer, to anaerobic fitness; from how he insists his players take opponents on one v one, to how he choreographs the way his team moves down the field in certain situations. Anson's theories, opinions and methods of coaching soccer, at times, are incredibly simple, and left me wondering why more coaches don't implement these methods. At other times, they are very sophisticated and complex, but always based on some simple aspect of the game.

There were times when I questioned if this book would ever be completed. I was working sixty-hour weeks on Soccer News — the soccer publication of which I am co-owner and editor. I was basically working on the book in my spare time, and I didn't have much. But several times, while I was in The Hut, I read a small sign on the bulletin board. The sign says: "You Can't Build A Reputation On What You Are *Going* To Do." Then, one day I was explaining to my then three-year-old daughter Allison how busy I was, and she said, "Why don't you just do all that so you won't have it to do anymore."

So I finished.

I would like to thank several people for their help. First of all, Anson for giving me the opportunity; my wife Cheri and daughter Allison for their patience and assistance; my partner Jan Cheves and her husband Carter for their help and encouragement; my parents Harry and Lorraine Nash and my brother Marty for their constant support.

Hope you enjoy it.

Preface

By Anson Dorrance

When I was growing up, I never had any preconceived notions that men and women were any different athletically. I did not have any real sports heroes, and I was never a good spectator. In my sports world people played, they didn't watch. Being raised abroad helped form this attitude and behavior because TV was not a part of our lives. I couldn't turn it on and see the great male athletes perform. And when I played, it was with my sister Maggie who was one year younger and a tremendous athlete. My mother was also a brilliant athlete. So when I started training women for the first time, I never had a condescending attitude about what they could and could not accomplish. Maggie had a competitive fury that was legendary in our home. I knew from playing with and against her that her pain threshold was at least comparable to the boys with which we played. I knew her physical courage was no different. As a result, I have never felt I had to coddle the young women that played for me. So when two players collide in practice and are obviously in pain, I do not select that time to show I care about them by rushing over to see if they are okay. I select that moment to show them I admire their physical courage and their ability to deal with the contact of our sometimes-violent sport.

When I was given the job to train and develop the women's soccer team at the University of North Carolina, I had high expectations. I also made a resolve from the beginning that I was going to take the work ethic and standards required to compete on the men's side of the Atlantic Coast Conference to this new women's team and do my best.

Next to creating a high level of intensity in practice, the greatest challenge in coaching women is to have high standards and to have a consistently ascending level of expectation. No one is ever good enough. Everyone can always improve, and practice sessions should be a stretch of each player's limits. With these challenges in mind, the constants in our practices at UNC are intensity, speed of play, attacking and defensive transition, tactical decision-making and training on your physical and technical edge. The following is a brief explanation of each and some critical points to keep in mind as you read through this book.

Intensity: Intensity is generally created by the Competitive Cauldron — playing to win. We record and rank everything we possibly can in each practice session, which allows our players to compete against each other every day. There are some environments that are not recorded, and in those cases the only effective way I know to make sure athletes are focused is to constantly nag — or coach — encourage, plead, drive and lead with stories of the great players of the past and how they were relentless in their ambition to be the best they could be.

It is also critical to establish standards, and they are set by highlighting the extraordinary moments in practice, if these moments ever occur. However, we have to wait for those moments to occur before we heap praise on the players or we will be settling for too low a standard. Never endorse what is below standard and your praise will have meaning. Never set a standard that can easily be achieved, and your expectations will create an environment where your athletes are on the edge of their game. It is time spent on this edge that improves your players. The truly great practices occur when we can keep them on this edge the longest.

Speed of Play: In the women's game, speed of play can never be fast enough. The standard is set for us, and it is the men's game. If you ever think your women's team is playing fast enough, go watch a boy's or men's game of comparable age and level immediately following your game. You will be shocked at how slow we are in areas that have nothing to do with physical gender differences. Our speed of technical preparation, speed of decision-making on the ball and anticipation off the ball is nowhere near where it could be if we just crank up our own environment to get closer to the men's game. It's not a mystery that many of our great national team players talk about how playing with boys when they were younger had a significant impact on their development. The impact was created by the environment forcing them to do everything so much quicker.

Transition: Like speed of play, attacking and defensive transition are water marks of your level as a team and your effectiveness as a coach. These qualities don't come naturally or comfortably for a player. Transition is a chance for the lazy player or lazy team to relax and hide from their responsibilities. The physical, psychological and tactical demands of high-level transition are significant. At the instant of possessional change, a player has a moment of physically wrenching acceleration or change of direction — whether or not they have the energy. Within that moment, the player has a menu of critical options they have to choose from in that split-second while they are exhausting themselves. During those periods of time, most players will take a break and most coaches will join them by not harping on it enough. As a result, our game suffers. Some players have a one-dimensional transition, and they become half-players by developing pride in their attacking transition or their defensive transition. Their coaches forgive them by placing them in thirds of the field where their lack of totality hurts the team the least. And the game suffers again.

Decision-Making: In teaching tactical decision-making, I believe in making sure every player understands the reasons for choosing every tactical option. I also believe it's important to appreciate that it's a choice because there are always alternatives. I encourage players that disagree with anything we are doing to come forward and recommend an alternative choice because I want every player sold on our system. Their belief in the system will make it work even more. If they have a better idea, they are encouraged to make their case to me. If it has merit, we go with it. We teach decision-making based on tactical clues — which third of the field the ball is in; whether the ball is on the flank or in the center; whether you are on attack or defense; whether you have numbers around the ball or are alone; whether the player on the ball can face or is marked closely; whether or not the defense is flat; whether or not the player on the ball has space or is pressured, and obviously many other factors. We have recommendations for the players based on our experience. But as long as the players are picking up the tactical clues of a situation, they have the freedom to improvise within the system and go outside of the recommended choice. We explore the depths of their knowledge and understanding with the Socratic method of teaching, and we often preface the question with "Future coaches of America ... " This plants the seed that they are developing an understanding of the game so that they, too, can eventually coach it.

Training on Your Physical and Technical Edge: We talked about this with the national team. We talk about it a lot at UNC, and we even talk about it in our summer camps. When we are doing the Coerver warmups, we encourage campers to train in that uncomfortable zone. They are changing directions so radically they are about to lose their balance. That is the physical edge. They are cutting the ball so quickly and sharply, they are just about to lose control. That is their technical edge.

Getting your team to transcend ordinary effort is the challenge in every training session and every match. I think when we are doing our best job at North Carolina, we are getting our players to apply extraordinary effort. I have been very proud of our consistent performance at UNC. In every match we play, there is a standard of intensity and effort that has not changed since the program began. In seasons when we have been very young, we certainly suffer. But the expectation of maximum personal effort from everyone we put on the field has not diminished. To get this effort, you as a coach are regularly dealing with the emotional strain of not accepting the lower standard of performance and effort. Your strength in coaching is having the courage to constantly deal with the athletes that unconsciously try to take things a bit easier. When I was a young coach, I used to feel that my practices were a great success when I could get through a session and things went smoothly.

So, invariably, I would pick training topics that were fun and easy to organize or coach, if you can call it that. And they were always successful. Of course, if there was always success, I was only training the players in areas in which they were already competent. And if the sessions were easy to coach, I was doing little to drive the players to their next level.

***

In late-1995, the USSF national staff coaches had a working symposium at the Nike headquarters near Portland, Oregon. I always enjoy the opportunity we are given to meet, and I always benefit from it. This gathering was no exception. With Tim Carter chairing a coaching committee, I was part of a group formalizing an observer program that Timo Liekoski had started. Timo had invited coaches that work in our player development structure to see first-hand what happens at the national level. This kind of observation has always been a part of coaching development, but what I enjoyed about formalizing the observer program was a chance to talk to members of the national staff about how we should direct our observers. This is an area where I think so many of us would benefit. After a while, your coaching development ceases to be about finding newer ways to organize practice. In other words, you soon stop collecting drills. Your development as a coach shifts to observing how the great ones motivate, lead or drive players to performances at higher and higher levels. I spent some time with UCLA coach Sigi Schmid discussing this. We talked about how if we observe the coach properly and not just his field coaching, we get into the fundamental aspects of his leadership. We are curious about what is said in practice and how it is said. But we are also curious about what happens off the field, on the bus going to practice, what is said in meetings, what relationships develop. We are basically looking to learn the parameters of your entire influence as a coach, leader, mentor and human being. I feel this is how you impact players if you are effectively coaching. And what are you creating — sometimes very consciously, but oftentimes covertly — as a theme for this group of people that play for you? Hopefully, high expectations, high standards, consistent effort and intensity, as well as a commitment to become the best they can be.

In the following chapters, we will explain how we try to develop high standards and expectations, how we get consistent effort from all of our players and how we get our players to make a commitment to become they best they can be.

Team Organization

Chapter 1

Greater Expectations

"Some coaches are no longer willing to make
the emotional commitment needed to motivate players
to attain the standard required of them
to compete successfully at the highest level.**"**

One of the opportunities I've had at UNC is to speak in different education classes and sports psychology classes. When I'm asked to speak, I always make it a point to get the course's reading list so I'm not entirely off-base. Looking through the required reading material of these classes forced me to see another discipline's perspective of coaching — how it is used in teaching academic material. It's interesting to see how educators look at coaching as just another way to convey their influence. They take a hazy area that coaching manuals and clinics don't treat in much detail, and they try to give it form.

Those are the issues I want to talk about in this chapter called "Greater Expectations." I think what happens to great coaches who are not as effective at the end of their career is they lose their willingness to take the required stress and emotional confrontation that they did when they were younger. All of us have watched the press excoriate these coaching legends as they try to follow their previous successes. I don't think there is any question about the knowledge of these coaches. I don't think these people know any less about their sport when they are losing their edge. I also don't think they lost their competitive fire. But what happens eventually in every professional leadership position — but maybe in the coaching profession more than most — is that some leaders no longer have the energy or willingness to make the emotional commitment to motivate people to attain the standard required of them to compete successfully at the highest level. Coaches sometimes are not willing to make that commitment because it's so exhausting. Maybe what you start to lack is energy, or maybe it is a kind of combative courage which you are sick of soliciting to fight the human tendency to be comfortably mediocre. There is an emotional battle that is constant when you are trying to take your players to higher levels, and your players are unconsciously fighting you to stay at a more comfortable level. All that is such a drain on us emotionally and psychologically that after a while we aren't willing to make that kind of sacrifice. We see brilliant men burn out regularly in our profession, and the editorials about these men ask the same question: What price did he pay for those achievements? Well, I believe the price high-profile football and basketball coaches pay is emotional and physical exhaustion from trying to keep themselves and the people in their programs on an impossible cutting edge. To constantly motivate players, you have to be a driving force and make personal investments for which you can pay dearly.

It is all described in a book we have named this chapter after — "Greater Expectations" by William Damon. The book jacket alone says a lot: "Overcoming the culture of indulgence in America's homes and schools." William Damon reviews issues about how educators and parents don't do enough and aren't demanding enough of the kids being taught and raised. In fact, many people have a misconstrued understanding of how to build self-esteem. One of the things he talks about in the book is that many parents and teachers want to create self-esteem, so they end up praising students or children for things that aren't really praise-worthy. The parent or teacher then loses credibility with the kids in whom they are trying to build confidence. Way down deep, the kids know the teacher or parent is just not telling them the truth. So in this noble ambition to build self-esteem, you often praise them for no real reason. It's a hollow kind of praise. We end up developing a lot of self-indulgent kids and students that don't have any standards, and we develop parents and teachers that don't have real respect.

I think it is a wonderful book. It displays a great mindset that all of us in the coaching profession should have. I've read a lot of books that have affected my coaching. But I haven't read a book that comes closer than this one to what all of us should be doing when we are developing people. It addresses the mistake all of us make. Part of the effort to build self-esteem gives the wrong message if we praise behavior that isn't praise-worthy. Sometimes, we aren't willing to make that emotional investment in our kids at home or in the kids we are teaching because to do so we have to be somewhat demanding and critical. It causes stressful moments of conflict, and that's a taxing price. Even in my own home, I can see what happens when my wife and I come home from a long day at work and are very tired. Donovan, our four-and-a-half-year-old son, has just been eating in front of the television, and he decides to leave his dish there and go play in his bedroom. Well, the correct behavior is for M'Liss or me to go find Donovan and say, "Donovan, your dish is sitting there in the living room, and that's not where you leave it. When you are finished eating, you bring it to the kitchen and put it in the dishwasher." Then there is a moment of confrontation with Donovan which is emotionally taxing — in a very small way. He will roll his eyes, object and say he'll do it later. Well, now you're getting a little angry because he's trying to blow you off, and it's not a very pleasant experience. It's not an issue about getting the dish in the dishwasher, but we are not in the mood for this type of dispute. And if we are the sort of parent, educator or coach who doesn't have the strength to constantly have these battles, we pick up the dish and put it in the dishwasher. Okay, now the dish is in the dishwasher, but Donovan has a lower standard of expectation.

This is what happens in the typical practice, and this is what happens with many coaches I observe. They are not willing to confront players when they are not exerting maximum effort and achieving maximum performance because it's a stressful, uncomfortable situation. They end up having a practice that is easy to run and fun to coach. And there are certainly no confrontations. Some of the young, inexperienced coaches in our summer soccer camp will have these happy-go-lucky practices where all the kids in their session are just having fun. Standards aren't being set because this young coach doesn't have the security yet to confront lower standards. So one of the challenges for me when I gather my camp coaches every night is to get the instructors to follow a demanding curriculum. The inexperienced coaches, however, figure out ways not to coach the demanding aspects of the curriculum. They don't want that conflict. They want a successful, stress-free, fun, recreational session. That doesn't mean a recreational type of session never has a place in a soccer camp. It does, of course, and I tell that to the staff. But great coaches are not afraid to tackle emotional situations in order to get players to accept a higher standard. And those are the people you pay big bucks. It's interesting that the inexperienced coach doesn't see yet that the experienced coach is doing a better job. They think, "Oh, clearly my session went so much better than his." But they don't see that the standard of their session was recreational as opposed to his, which was achieving an understanding or an experience at a much higher level.

This is just like what is happening in modern America, where both parents go off to work and come home exhausted. Rather than confront the issue of strict parenting and having high standards, we go the route of grabbing the dish, throwing it in the dishwasher and ignoring Donovan. And Donovan grows up being the self-indulgent, spoiled individual that has never had to do anything for himself because his parents have done things for him all his life. His parents have told him he's a great kid, and he thinks he is a great kid. But he thinks his parents are weak and insincere because they praise him for whatever he does. That's the way the lower-level coach eventually loses the respect of his team — by not being demanding enough, not harping on a higher standard and not making the stressful, passionate investment and risk a loss of popularity. They win the popularity contest, but sacrifice respect. The result is that the standards are lowered. And before you know it, you don't have a team of high achievers, you don't have high standards and you have lowered your sights as a coach. The coaches think they are building confidence and self-esteem in their players, and all they are really doing is lowering a standard. That doesn't mean you should never encourage someone who has made a good effort, but you've got to balance it. And this ability to know when and how to confront a player or a team and when to back off or show unconditional support is the unique juggling act that our profession requires.

All of us can survive one or two moments of conflict. But it is the constant battle against mediocrity that's stressful in coaching. All of us have a tendency to gravitate to an easier level. The successful coaches fight that tendency constantly. Part of your persona as a coach is motivating your players to select their free time to develop themselves. For example, a player who stays fit year-round ... someone somewhere along this athlete's career path affected them. No one jumps out of the womb thinking, "Yeah, I'm going to be twelve-months fit." Somewhere along that path, someone encouraged this young athlete to have discipline, and it was an emotional investment by that person. From an individual perspective, the fight against mediocrity is taxing. It is even more taxing from a leadership perspective, where you can't just take care of yourself, you have to inspire the ones around you to follow your example.

There has to be a presence of higher standards, a presence of greater expectations. That's the ultimate challenge of high-level coaching. And by high-level coaching, I don't mean the national team coach or the professional level coach. It can be the great youth coach, the great senior coach, the great whatever coach. The key is to have a balance. You have to choose your battles and know when to challenge the player. There are times when it might not be an easy or popular environment for you to challenge them, but there are times when they are just going to have to suck it up and deal with it. You can't be forever sensitive to their moods. And, trust me, the standards most players set for themselves will usually be in a comfort zone that is well below their potential.

Chapter 2

The Balancing Act

"In our program, we try to maintain a balance between furious competition and light-heartedness."

It's interesting, when you're asked to give lectures at the United States Soccer Federation coaching schools, they want you to stress that there are all different kinds of coaches. At these lectures, we emphasize that you should always coach through your own personality. I think if you coach that way, you are more sincere.

We all adopt mentors and people we admire, and we try to emulate aspects of their particular coaching style. But if you try to emulate someone who has a coaching style far removed from your own personality, your style is not going to come through with any kind of sincerity. And it probably won't be effective. If it's not a part of what you are as a person and as a coach, it will not be sincere. It's going to be a very hollow coaching style. If you want to be effective, you have to find aspects of your personality to coach through. All athletes and coaches like to say they are very competitive people. But everyone is always so quick to point out they are not overly competitive, like if they really try to win it's a personality disorder. I certainly would like to say that I am very competitive. I have never looked at competition in any sort of negative light. I don't feel like I have to qualify it. For me, the competition itself is the only thing in which I am competitive. Once the competition is over, it isn't an issue anymore. And I think winning and losing gracefully is critical. In our program, we try to maintain a balance between furious competition and a light-heartedness because there can be all kinds of negative spin-offs from competition. It can shatter team chemistry. It can create an environment that is oppressive. And what I like about what has happened over the years here at North Carolina is that we have figured out a way to make the practice environments unbelievably competitive. But the rest of the time — even when the drill is over and the young women are jogging to the water fountain — it's lighter. We figured out a way to maintain that balance because I've seen other people adopt a competitive mentality that creates an incredibly oppressive regime. The whole thing — from beginning to end, day-in, day-out — is so competitive it's depressing.

You have to have a balance, especially when you are training young women. They have a tremendous capacity to compete, but competing is not the end-all for them. You have to figure out when to pull back from it and lighten up the training environment. I don't want to give the impression that we have a depressing atmosphere here. If people came to our training sessions, they would be impressed with the intensity, but they would also be impressed with the light atmosphere. That's what's critical in this juggling act. All the players constantly have to have a sense that you enjoy their company. If you can figure out a way to crack jokes even about the most morbid situations in practice, it helps. One of the neatest things about athletics is a lot of it is real comedy — people banging into each other, falling on their heads — and you've got to figure out a way to make light of all that. Competition is an underlying theme to what we do at UNC, but there are a lot of other themes as well. If we used competition as the only aspect of what we do here, we'd be missing the point. In fact, the players don't talk about it. Those are not the memories they take with them. I remember one time Keri Sanchez and I were invited to be on the ACC Hotline radio show, and we talked about the program here. Keri was asked a question point-blank. Mick Mixon, the host, said, "Pretend Anson isn't here, and tell us what you have learned most from the program at UNC?" Keri said, "Most of the things I've taken from the program have nothing to do with soccer. They have to do with life and relationships. Anson is always telling us that soccer is just a game, and it's no big deal. As a result, we don't feel a whole lot of pressure about the game, and what we come away with is an attitude that what is critical is that we try."

Competition is something that is woven into the fabric of our player development. But it is not what the players feel, and that's what is important. When I talk about our competitive structure in clinics or lectures, it intimidates some coaches. They feel there is no way their kids will enjoy this type of environment because the only thing the coaches draw from it is competition and testing. But I do want to emphasize that one of the biggest problems I see when I watch most training sessions, is a lack of intensity. You just don't develop when you train without intensity. But you have to balance intensity and competition with a light-heartedness about athletics itself. It's not that big a deal. It's just a game. It always amuses me when I get an urgent phone call. How could I get an urgent phone call about soccer? There is nothing urgent in what we are doing here. Sometimes in athletics, we give everyone the impression that we are doing something of tremendous importance, but it's not really all that important. I think you can get a heck of a lot out of athletics if you approach it with the attitude that you have a chance to get close to a group of people, develop a kind of discipline, be goal-oriented. You can draw a lot from that. There is also the opportunity to see what you are like because if there are any kind of profound revelations in athletics, it's that you are seen at your best and at your worst. There is nothing hidden. Even though athletics is artificial, it takes you through an incredible range of personal emotions that are very real. If you have the capacity to detach yourself from it, athletics is almost a study of yourself — Am I disciplined or do I just intend to be? Am I a team player or do I hope the starter screws up so I can play more? Do I panic? Am I selfish? Do I have physical courage? It's like a laboratory of the human spirit. It's an artificial environment, but it still serves to highlight almost every human quality. You feel things that are very real. But you can never take it too seriously, and you can never take yourself too seriously because the environment you are in is not very real at all.

One thing that's neat about the young women we get here at UNC is that they develop a wonderful humility. Obviously, their freshman year does it to them because wherever they came from, they were God's Gift to the Game. When they come in here, they're just crushed because everyone is so competitive. It's tough for them to stand out. Even the greatest players — players like April Heinrichs, who even as a freshman was a dominant player — don't feel like they stood out. I can remember April talking about her freshman season, saying how tough it was for her to demonstrate her ability. And I was thinking, "April, are you kidding me? What are you talking about? You came in here and tore it up immediately." In my mind, there was nothing humble about her performance as a freshman. But she had never been in an environment where she had to work so hard to gain so little dominance. For her, it was humbling. That experience, fortunately, is something that all these women carry with them. One of the worst things about athletics is that it can create such enormous egos. But we don't take things seriously enough here for anyone to develop that big of an ego. And fortunately, our traditions here at UNC have had such incredible champions in the past that it's difficult for anyone to presume to be any better than someone who was here before them. So it creates a wonderful environment for personal growth, as well as athletic development, without delusions of grandeur. Those are the aspects of the program I enjoy the most. But when you are aspiring to develop excellence, the competitive cauldron is what will take you there, and that's an emphasis of our program. Those, however, would never be my memories, and they would not be the memories of the women who play here.

The traditions at the University of North Carolina — the records and streaks — are not something we compete against. They are just products. We never talk about streaks and records. Obviously, though, in the back of some players' minds they have their own agendas. And that's fine. If a player wants to be the career leading scorer in the NCAA, great. But it will never be anything I would suggest. Obviously, I would like my front-runners to score goals in buckets, but it's not going to be an idea I place in their mind. We have goal-setting meetings three times a year, and the players select things to achieve. Part of each meeting is how many goals and assists they want to get in the season. Other goals may be making the Sports Festival, or the U.S. National Team, or the national team player pool. We want the players to be goal-oriented, and the ones that are goal-oriented develop the most. There's no question about that. With some players, though, you don't even have a goal-setting meeting because they struggle to set goals, they never reach the goals they set, and that becomes a factor in their unhappiness. So we just talk about what's going on in their lives. I just don't think you should force everyone to set goals. Some people don't like to set goals, because they are afraid of not achieving them. I'm not going to sit here and play psychiatrist and try to bend them into a position in which I feel more comfortable. It's ridiculous to construct an organization of one kind of personality. Your life is going to be filled with all kinds of people, and so will your team. If someone is not comfortable setting goals, fine. Let's go in their direction and let them set their own agenda. What do they want to get out of all this?

One year, a player came into my office and said, "I want to have a good time every time I come to practice." That was her goal. Once we set that goal, it was very interesting watching her come to practice. Sure enough, she showed up with a wonderful kind of freedom and just had a good time. That was good enough for me. She contributed tremendously to team chemistry. Everyone liked her. I liked her. She wasn't a world-beater on the field, but she didn't have to be. That wasn't her goal.

Chapter 3

The Competitive Cauldron

❝We give our players the best outside competition available, but I also firmly believe in setting up a competitive cauldron in practice.**❞**

Something I take great pride in here at UNC is that over the course of four years a player improves dramatically, and I think there are a lot of reasons. One reason is that we play an unbelievably ambitious schedule. We don't duck anyone. We go all over the country to play the best teams, and there's no question that this type of competition further develops the athletes we have here. Take a typical team here at UNC and look at the number of top-twenty teams each kid has played against by the time she's a senior. It's a very high number relative to any other program in the country. The schedule we play is designed to be very difficult. The most wonderful example of this is the team we took out West in 1992. In four days, we played four top-twenty teams back-to-back-to-back-to-back. It was just a tremendous run. We had another insane run during the Fall of 1995. We had graduated one of the greatest recruiting classes in our history, losing seven starting caliber players, many of them national caliber — Dawn Crow, Danielle Egan, Shelly Finger, Angie Kelly, Keri Sanchez, Roz Santana and Tisha Venturini. In 1995, we played six games in eleven days, starting with William & Mary and Notre Dame, finishing with Virginia and playing Duke and two first-year programs, Florida and Florida State, in the middle. It was designed to stretch our young team. Those kinds of experiences harden our players. And certainly, a contributing factor in our schedule strength is that generally we go so far in the NCAA Tournament. Even the nature of our conference develops us. We're always playing additional top-twenty teams because the ACC Tournament takes us through the cream of the conference after having faced them earlier in the regular season. And year-in, year-out, the best in the conference are nationally ranked. So every year, we're playing an extraordinary number of competitive teams.

We give our players the best outside competition available. But I also firmly believe in setting up a competitive cauldron in practice because outside competition, no matter how challenging, cannot be the only environment where players are pushed. No matter how often you play, you will still spend more time in practice. And that is where your players always get their edge. Our practice environment is competitive because we keep score in everything we can. We stole this from UNC basketball coach Dean Smith. When I was a young coach, I used to watch his practices, and I was always impressed with how well organized his practices were. The part I was impressed with most was how every player is assessed in practice every day for everything he does. Every time he shoots and misses, it's recorded. And there's a shooting percentage for each player at the end of every practice. Every time he plays a three v three or a five v five or a half-court matchup, there's a record of a win and a loss. I wouldn't doubt it if they were even recording matchups in a five v five, showing how each player matched up with each other player. So every player in the course of a Dean Smith practice is assessed every step of the way. And we do the same thing. We record everything. Every player is assessed in every aspect of the game in practice — and we end up with her overall practice performance for the year. I can look at the charts and see there's a direct correlation between the best players on the team and their rank on these charts. It doesn't always end up pure, and that has to do with the fact that I have not been able to rank heading appropriately. But as with everything else, the matrix is evolving, and hopefully, we will eventually solve the inequity. But the order of rank is always very, very close to being the way I would rank my players subjectively. And by the way, I'm still learning from Dean Smith. I asked him if I could attend all the practices before the 1996 ACC basketball tournament. Since we lost in 1995, I needed to watch him work again.

Our final composite ranking is compiled by Tom Sander, my veteran manager, at the end of the season. On our bulletin board, for everyone to see, is a field player rank in every competitive category. It stays on the wall the entire year. On page thirty, we have provided the 1994 season's practice performance chart to show the twenty-three field players' final ranking and the final ranking of our four goalkeepers. (We have omitted the names of the players at the bottom half of the list.) As a comparison, on page thirty-one we show our 1995 rankings to show the additions to the process and the evolution of the matrix. It also shows player improvement from one year to the next. A good example of incredible improvement is Vanessa Rubio. Her improvement from 1994 to 1995 was dramatic, and her play in many important matches in '95 reflected a new work ethic and the commitment she made in the spring and summer of 1995. We use rank within the team as a reference point as opposed to a decathlon point system because practice competition within

1994 Final Statistical Composite Rankings •••••

Category	Aerobic Fitness			Anaerobic	1v1's	1v1's to Goal			3 T Shooting	Heading	Tri. Passing	Speed	M. Competitive		
Sub-Category	Cooper	120's	Cones			Off/Def	Offensive	Defensive							
Sub-Cat Multiplier	1X	1/2X	1/2X			1X	1/2X	1/2X							
Category Multiplier		2X		1X	2X	1X	1X		1X	1/2X	1/2X	2X	2X	Total Pts.	Rank
Rank Player															
1. Keller, Debbie	3	1	1	4	1	4			5	13	13	13	4	66.0	1.
2. Sanchez, Keri	1	1	1	1	9		12	1	10	15	19	2	6	70.5	2.
3. Venturini, Tisha	7	1	1	3	7		8	3	7	8	6	21	3	71.5	3.
4. Wilson, Staci	9	1	1	9	6	6			4	20	1	9	2	73.5	4.
5. Egan, Danielle	3	1	1	8	2		3	13	13	6	12	5	9	74.0	5.
6. Confer, Robin	12	5	10	2	4	10			3	1	19	8	12	92.5	6.
7. Santana, Rosalind	8	10	5	11	3	4			12	22	2	12	8	100.5	7.
8. Kelly, Angela	3	1	1	21	5		13	14	1	17	18	18	11	107.0	8.
9. Dacey, Sarah	11	15	1	12	14	6			2	9	13	14	5	116.0	9.
10. Roberts, Amy	3	1	1	5	10	11			16	14	9	7	18	117.5	10.
10. Uritus, Meg	12	5	5	17	10		1	2	6	4	4	17	9	117.5	10.
12. Player 12	2	1	1	10	10	9			15	22	6	10	14	119.0	12.
13. Player 13	16	15	2	15	10	2			7	12	4	6	20	128.5	13.
14. Player 14	17	10	15	14	19	5			22	3	6	22	1	137.0	14.
15. Player 15	12	15	10	23	14	7			16	18	3	15	7	138.0	15.
16. Player 16	17	10	20	16	20	5			11	10	22	1	18	158.0	16.
17. Player 17	21	15	1	19	16	9			7	5	9	16	15	165.0	17.
18. Player 18	22	20	5	13	8		11	12	14	16	13	23	16	181.5	18.
19. Player 19	20	15	1	7	18	15			23	11	9	20	12	183.0	19.
20. Player 20	12	15	5	18	17	8			18	22	13	11	22	183.5	20.
21. Rubio, Vanessa	17	20	5	20	22	7			20	21	23	4	17	184.5	21.
22. Player 22	23	10	1	22	21	10			21	7	19	3	23	188.5	22.
23. Player 23	10	15	1	6	23	14			19	2	13	19	21	190.5	23.

Rank Keeper															
1. Noonan, Tracy	2			1	1				4				2	13.0	1.
2. Finger, Shelly	3			2	2				1				3	16.0	2.
3. Keeper 3	3			4	3				2				1	18.0	3.
4. Keeper 4	1			3	4				3				4	22.0	4.

·····● 1995 Final Statistical Composite Rankings

Category	Aerobic Fitness			Anaerobic	1v1's	1v1's to Goal			3T Shooting	Tri. Passing	Long Service	Heading		Speed	M. Competitive	Total Pts.	Rank
Sub-Category	Cooper	120's	Cones			Off/Def	Offensive	Defensive				Long Serve	Ladder				
Sub-Cat Multiplier	1X	1/2X	1/2X			1X	1/2X	1/2X				1/2X	1/2X				
Category Multiplier	2X			1X	3X	1X	1X		1X	1/2X	1/2X	1X		2X	2 1/2X		
Rank Player																	
1. Parlow, Cindy	3	2	1	19	5		3	7	13	1	8	1	1	5	1	74.5	1.
2. Keller, Debbie (1)	5	1	2	8	5	5			3	5	7	6	10	11	3	81.0	2.
3. Confer, Robin (6)	18	1	10	9	2	1			13	8	1	6	6	3	5	81.5	3.
4. Wilson, Staci (4)	10	1	10	9	1	1			10	3	16	13	16	8	7	96.0	4.
5. Falk, Aubrey (13)	11	1	10	15	4		6	7	1	8	3	8	8	1	12	96.5	5.
6. Karvelsson, Rakel	1	1	10	9	10		2	2	16	10	4	10	5	9	2	101.0	6.
7. Roberts, Tiffany	4	1	1	1	3		4	6	19	14	11	19	12	2	13	103.5	7.
8. Fettig, Nel (15)	8	3	10	5	8	3			5	1	2	8	20	15	9	104.5	8.
9. Uritus, Meg (10)	15	3	4	20	7		8	5	4	15	8	3	2	13	4	107.0	9.
10. Roberts, Amy (10)	7	1	1	3	9	13			2	10	8	2	11	6	16	120.5	10.
11. Rubio, Vanessa	20	4	10	9	12		9	9	6	10	14	17	14	4	6	137.5	11.
12. Player 12	16	5	9	17	11		10	14	8	7	11	4	9	12	8	146.5	12.
13. Player 13	6	1	10	6	15		7	10	7	10	17	13	19	16	11	151.0	13.
14. Player 14	9	1	10	4	14	17			15	18	14	20	13	7	10	164.0	14.
15. Player 15	1	1	1	18	18	12			12	4	6	10	4	10	14	165.0	15.
16. Player 16	17	15	10	16	13	11			20	16	11	13	3	17	19	201.5	16.
17. Player 17	14	3	5	2	17	15			18	17	17	12	7	14	18	203.5	16.
18. Player 18	19	15	10	9	16		11	4	9	5	5	18	18	20	15	205.5	18.
19. Player 19	11	1	6	6	19		13	12	11	19	20	4	15	18	20	216.0	19.
20. Player 20	11	11	3	9	20		14	16	17	20	19	16	17	19	17	235.5	20.
Rank Keeper																	
1. Noonan, Tracy (1)	1			1					1						3	12.5	1.
2. Mullinix, Siri	3			2					2						1	13.5	2.
3. Keeper 3	2			4					4						2	23.0	3.
4. Keeper 4	4			3					3						4	26.0	4.

Notes: Final rankings for each category are indicated in boxes (1 to 23)
Ranking is multiplied by multiplier (importance of category)
All categories' multiplied scores are added for total

*Central players (Uritus, Sheppard, Fettig, Hutton) have multiplier of 1X; Dacey has 1.5X

the team is always going to be the critical factor in match playing time. And it all gets back to the core principle of the competitive cauldron. Also, with the annual evolution of the matrix, player-vs-player ranking is the simplest way to generate positive competition in practice sessions, creating the intensity necessary for optimum player development. In the player matrix, we don't give equal weight to every competition. We consider speed, one v one ability and a player's impact in all the small-sided games to carry the greatest weight, and the category multipliers reflect this.

[Our new computer match analysis, which is included at the end of this book, ranks our opponents according to how they compare to every other team on the schedule – like in our player matrix – in the categories we have selected to highlight. Ultimately, I would like to develop a standard: win/loss percentage in the defensive, middle and attacking thirds of the field. Those would be the standards for what we expect from each position or group, but this will take more data. In 1995, however, I wanted to know in which areas our opponents were most successful against us, and which opponents gave us the most problems. Then we would try to improve in those areas. I also want to know our standards of performance in every match so we can compete against the always-challenging demands of the game itself, which can sometimes be harder to beat than the opponent.]

The first competition the players face upon returning to practice in the Fall is the Cooper Run, which is how far you can run in twelve minutes. It's a test of aerobic conditioning. With aerobic fitness, we evaluate the players competitively in three fitness arenas, and the arena in which we put them changes as the season wears on. We do the Cooper Test the first couple of weeks of practice. Early in the season, we do one-hundred-and-twenty-yard runs. Near the end of the season, we do cones. We also have an anaerobic fitness component in which we evaluate the players in a series of twenty- and forty-yard sprints. We set that up based on a speed ladder. The speed rating is just a ranking in pure speed in a forty-yard dash. With one v ones, we do two different kinds. The first is one v ones to goal, which is a player taking on a defender when the defender serves a goal kick. The defender is on the six-yard box, and the attacking player is on the mid-stripe. The defender serves a goal kick, and the attacker cleans it up and sprints it up to the defender, who comes out to meet her. In this, they're evaluated in four different ways. One is if the defender stuffs the player. Obviously, that's the ultimate victory for the defender, and she gets four points. If the attacking player doesn't beat the defender one v one but gets a shot off and it goes wide, the defender gets three points. If the shot is on the face of the goal, two points. If the defender is beaten on the dribble, the defender goes down to one point. If the attacking player scores, the defender gets nothing. The other one v ones are just using cones as goals. Both players attack and defend the same cone. As often as possible, our strikers are playing with regulation goals and active keepers. Finishing against goalkeepers into regulation goals puts a positive pressure on everyone in the exercise – the player trying to finish, the defender and the keeper. This is why we always try to carry four goalkeepers on our roster. We try to recruit two and encourage two to walk on from the campus population. That way, we can have two of these games with live keepers. It's an excellent environment. Three-tiered shooting is just a shooting exercise we do that's recorded. Heading is still evolving. In 1994, it was just a one v one heading drill. In 1995, we threw in an additional heading element – heading for distance. Triangle passing is a passing organization drill where they're evaluated on their ability to string flighted passes together. All of these drills are explained in detail in chapter sixteen

We try to create a competitive cauldron in all the training environments, which is also what we try to create with our schedule. We try to create as much competition as possible in the four v fours, five v fives, three v threes, and even in the eleven v eleven, starters vs reserves scrimmage at the end of training. All the games are recorded, and we post it on the wall. They see it everyday – wins, loses and ties. All the categories are reworked after every practice by the manager, who rearranges the rankings in all the categories. At the end of the season, it's all tabulated, as you can see on pages thirty-one and thirty-two. There are practices, however, where we don't do everything on the matrix. We want to make some practices recreational, like a pre-game day where we might not do anything that is recorded. In these situations, we do low-energy, non-competitive, team-building exercises that still require focus and technique. However, these exercises don't knock them around physically or psychologically. We want to taper them physically and emotionally going into a game. The coaches don't talk about the charts too much because we don't want everything to be oppressive. We try to be relaxed and laid-back about everything, except when the training begins. Then there is a fury of intensity. We just put the charts on the wall. The kind of player who wants to be a champion will fight to the top of that ladder. If she doesn't want to be a champion, her ranking will not affect her. You are just not going to motivate them to move up the ladder unless they want to compete. What players basically need is a challenge, and the charts are another challenge for them. If they are at the bottom of the ladders, they think maybe they should work harder. It will also objectively showcase their weaker areas. If they have a lot of pride and competitive spirit, they will fight to the top of the ladder or spend more time in areas that need work. The only time we talk about the charts is in our player conferences. We look at areas where they can improve and ask them if they would like to be more competitive in that particular area. If they say they would, then it's their goal to improve. Not ours. We will share everything we can with them to help them get better. The desire to be the best should always be present, and the charts are a reminder. That's why they stay on the wall year-round.

Rosalind Santana:

"As I went along, I found it easier to compete in practices. Now it's just natural. In fact, it's so natural I can't think of any other way."

When I came here, I wasn't really expected to do anything. Anson told me straight forward that I wouldn't play until my sophomore year. That excited me more. I was like, "Who does he think he is? I'm playing!" I started the second game of the season and kept starting until I left.

The strangest thing is that when I came here, I thought I'd leave just as a better soccer player. Of course, that happened. I grew tremendously soccer-wise. But I'll take much more with me, especially my competitive edge. People are just amazed about how I'll never settle for second best. I got that mentality here. We never entered a season thinking that maybe we'll take second this year. We always approached it like, "Are we going to be national champions or not?" And we were going to work as hard as we possibly could to be national champions.

There was a lot of hard work involved, especially every day in practice. Getting up for games is easy. Obviously, you are going to be competitive in games. No one has to be too competitive to enter a game and want to win. But the extra edge we have in practice is what's important. Almost everything we do in practice is recorded, and every week we see where we stand. And who wants to be at the bottom of the list? In practice, there is just no room for not trying your hardest, and it's due to Anson. The first day I got here and from then on, I just tried my hardest in practice. That's just the way it is. When you see players working so hard, you want to work just as hard. The upperclassmen expect it from you, but you have to prove to them that you belong on the field.

As I went along, I found it easier to compete in practices. Now it's just natural. In fact, it's so natural I can't think of any other way. It's just aggravating to me when people don't try as hard in practice as they would in games. It's hard for me to understand why someone would step on the field if they are not going to make a total commitment. That attitude is something I now have for life. That's the way I am now, and I think it's great.

This is something I didn't know before I came: Anson doesn't take you into his office and say, "You're not trying hard enough." It's just something that happens, and it doesn't happen overnight. If you don't want to try hard, you really don't have to. Everyone thinks that our team is made up of thirty of the best players in the country and everyone is an amazing soccer player. That's just not true. We have different levels, and at our own levels everyone is working very hard and making everyone better.

I was the assistant coach at Chapel Hill High School, and I had this girl who enrolled at UNC. I heard from the coach that she wasn't trying out for the team here. I asked her why, and she said, "I can't make that team. I'm not good enough." That's sad to me. I just finished four years here, and for anyone to have the opportunity to be on such an incredible team ... how can they not give it a chance? It's such an amazing experience. I'm a much more confident person now. I know that I have worked hard and accomplished a lot. When I interviewed for jobs, they said, "Tell me about your team." And I just went on forever.

Chapter 4

Learning How And Why

"In four years, all of our players are basically
ready to coach because they not only understand the game,
they have an understanding
of how to verbally explain the game.**"**

I was raised a Catholic, and a catechism is a litany that's pounded into you through memorization. Our pre-game ritual is almost a catechism. When you're a young catholic, I don't think you understand anything you memorize, but there it is in your brain. You have no understanding of it, but all of these words and phrases are in there. As you gain understanding, all of a sudden these things you've memorized gain meaning.

We have the same kind of system. Our players have a great memorization of what to say back to me in pre-game before they really understand it. But what happens over the course of the four years – because they're seeing the situations so many times and being regularly quizzed about them – they start to understand. We use the Socratic method constantly in our teaching. One reason we use this method is I went to law school, and I can remember how incredibly focused I was in every law class because of the Socratic method. There's a wonderful kind of social pressure in the Socratic method that is very effective. No one wants to be humiliated. So when you ask a question to the team, the Socratic method, if used correctly, involves everyone, not just the one person answering the question. You don't say, "Debbie, what about the balancing forward? Where should she position herself?" When you say that, everyone in the room falls asleep except Debbie. They are not involved in answering the question, so they stop listening. But if you say, "What is the position of the balancing forward in this situation ... Debbie?" You pause between the question and who you assign to answer it so everyone feels they might be called. Now, everyone in the room has answered the question in their minds because they're afraid you're going to ask them. Through the Socratic method everyone has to answer every question you ask before you assign it to someone. It's wonderful. They know they're going to be called on eventually. They watch other people get humiliated because they haven't given a correct answer, or watch them gain respect if they nail a question with confidence and flair. The humiliation is not deliberate, though. In fact, it can be done with wonderful humor because we don't take ourselves too seriously. You don't really tear them apart the way you might in a law school environment. But it's intimidating nonetheless. No one wants to not know the answer. And the ones that are most intimidated, obviously, are the freshmen because they don't know the answers. You have to call on them periodically to let them know they're not immune and they had better learn as quickly as they can. There is no greater pressure for an undergraduate soccer player than to ask her a question about a game she has played most of her life and have her give an answer in front of her peers. We get great focus from our players that way.

It's funny, if you ask someone that doesn't know the answer, the players around her will try to give her the answer. They'll whisper it to her, and someone else's answer ends up coming back to you. Then, of course, you continue to probe to see how little they actually understand in the answer. Everyone wants everyone else to know the answer, so there's a wonderfully quick learning process. And one thing that's neat about the kids that come through this program – in four years all of them are basically ready to coach because not only do they have an understanding of the game, they have an understanding of how to verbally explain the game. I think that is one reason we have been successful in placing so many young women in the coaching profession. They are very confident when they get out in front of a group. I tell them they are going to be amazed at how much they know and how clearly they can express it. All of our players come here without too much of an understanding of our system. A lot of players come in as wonderful players with unbelievable talent, but they certainly don't have an understanding of how to express what they know. A lot of great players don't really understand how to verbally express the timing of their run, even though they understand how to perform it. Here, they learn how to express it. We are going to ask them, and they are going to have to tell us back. The ones that really know how to make the run could possibly say, "I don't know but I'll be there, don't worry about it." And they will. But that's not good enough. They can't get away with that here. They have got to give the litany of when the run should be made. All the players that have been trained in my system can express everything verbally because they are asked to do it all the time. They have it organized in their mind. They just know it. To begin with, you have to communicate it to them, and there is a process involved in expressing these concepts to the players. Initially, when you communicate a tactic, you try to break it down to its barest element, giving the tactical clues on which decisions are based. From this most basic, small-group level – whatever the tactic – we build it up into a small game and then ultimately into the big game. We play a lot of eleven v eleven choreography, which means the goalkeeper has the ball, and she throws it out to the left back. The left back knocks it up to the left midfielder, then you have the flooding of zones. You knock it into the right wing who is in the center. She drops it back to the center half, who finds the right midfielder over the top. The right midfielder goes endline, serves a bending flighted ball into the box to the back post and the box is organized by having a player at the near post, one at the far post, and one in the slot. We do a lot of that all the way down the field, and the other team does the same thing coming back. We do this choreography – where the players don't have a choice as to where to serve the ball – back and forth, eleven v eleven. So you're teaching them in the eleven v eleven environment. You tell them, "These are the runs and these are your choices." It's out of that basic shape and movement choreography that your game flows.

When we play eleven v eleven, I stop it when something needs to be corrected, obviously. But I'm always stopping when I see something particularly brilliant. I try to stop it more when there's success. When there's success, we bring the group together and tell them exactly what they did right. We say, "Yes that's the way the game is played. If we play like that, we'll beat everyone." You have to continually reinforce all the things they do properly. It's not that they don't know when things have gone well. However, the nice thing about articulating it is you're emphasizing the exact reason why that particular situation was so perfect. By doing this, you're clarifying the point exactly, and you never know when the light bulb goes on. You have to share the precise tactical reasons for the success. After a while, "Great Stuff!" is not expansive enough. Everyone learns at different speeds and everyone might learn during a different day. When you bring the group together, you never know which player is finally realizing what you're talking about.

Once they have an understanding of movement and positions, their speed of play increases. One of the distinguishing qualities about good teams is their speed of play, which is your ability to move the ball quickly through the other team. And a part of speed of play is speed of decision-making. It is also speed of movement off the ball, speed of organization around the ball. It involves a lot of running off the ball and quick decisions on the ball. A soccer game has an infinite number of situations, and you're never going to totally review all of them in practice. What you try to do, though, is give them a basic structure and let their creativity flow out of it. For instance, when you're flooding zones up top, you're telling them you want all your strikers on one side of the field. Now, once they're on that side of the field, there are some general pieces of advice to give them – when to show for a pass and when to run at the restraining line. But the environment is changing constantly. The angles of reception and the angles of pressure are changing. There are an infinite variety of supporting angles and distances and runs they can make. It's all based on so many other factors – like pressuring player distance, angle of pressure and speed of approach. So you can't choreograph everything and, of course, you don't want to. But, if you give them general tendencies, coach these tendencies and watch their creativity flow out of a general framework, then you're getting somewhere.

When you see something particularly creative and effective, you reinforce it immediately, especially if it is something counter to a fundamental coaching principle you were teaching. If they get away with it, you let them know that what they did was unbelievably skillful, but in that particular situation, the odds of them succeeding aren't good, so that probably wasn't a good decision. Tell them, "Your skill got you out of there, but there's no guarantee that your skill is always going to get you out of that situation." For example, dribbling out of your own defensive penalty box ... the rewards for making that decision are very low. Now you have your sweeperback with possession on her own eighteen-yard line. Now you're nowhere. She could have been stripped, and the ball could be in the back of the net. So there was no reason for her to take that risk, whereas a forward on the edge of the other team's penalty box taking a player on has wonderful potential. Now the ball could be shot in the back of the other team's net, and there is no risk if she's stripped on the edge of their penalty box. They have another hundred yards to go before they even get to your goal. So you're teaching them to constantly know the reward-risk factor, and it's all within your teaching context. Even if your sweeper can beat a player in her own box, you reprimand her at halftime or after the game because it just wasn't worth the risk, even though she got away with it. But if a player on the edge of the attacking penalty box is looking to pass, you reprimand her because passing in that instance has so many variables. The only excuse to pass the ball in the attacking third with one player to beat is if your pass results in a first-time shot on goal from a better angle. She has to take the risk and responsibility to beat the player herself. The players, however, are not the only ones with responsibilities. As coaches, we have to give precise information on how we want things done, but also to be able to defend our reasoning.

Chapter 5

Respecting Opponents

❝We feel the greatest respect
we can afford a team is by crushing them.**❞**

At the University of North Carolina, our challenge is to try to live up to an impossible tradition. Layered under the grand tradition of striving to be the perennial national champion are the many other traditions that help us get there. Almost as impossible as winning consistently is trying to intelligently answer questions about it in a sentence or two without reviewing everything and everyone from our past that got us there. "Coach, do you consider your team a dynasty?" How do you answer that question gracefully? A reporter from Greensboro asked me that question, and here's what I tried to escape with: "If people want to consider us a dynasty, I want them to understand it's a dynasty of year-round play. It's a dynasty of commitment to being the best, and it's a dynasty of hard work."

Those are the only dynastic aspects we can preserve every year because there's no guarantee we're going to win on the field. No guarantee at all. People who don't understand winning, don't understand how fragile it is. They assume that winning is something we take for granted. We never do. People assume we think we're going to win every game automatically, and that's not true. When you don't respect an opponent, you get beaten. We go into every game with tremendous respect for our opponent. Because we win, people get the impression we don't have any respect for the teams we beat. That's a myth. Sometimes following a close game, I'll read that the other coach or the other players have said, "I hope they respect us now." That always disappoints me. We respect everyone. That's why we are consistent. We feel the greatest respect we can afford a team is by crushing them. That shows we respected them enough to be up for the game and respected them enough to go after them. I think when you don't chase and bury a team, you are showing a lack of respect for yourself and the team you are playing. That's always been a part of our pre-game philosophy. We don't go into any game with any kind of overconfidence. Part of the reason for that lack of overconfidence is that we respect more than just the teams we play. We also understand that we're always competing against elements beyond the opponent. Obviously, you compete against the other team, but you always compete against the game, too. And the game is sometimes harder to beat than the other team. The game is unbelievable. All of us as spectators, players and coaches have seen, participated in or coached games where a team outshot an opponent 40-1 and lost 1-0. When that happens, the opposition hasn't beaten you. The 40-1 totals show you that. All that's beaten you that day is the game itself. That's the nature of soccer, and it should keep everyone who coaches and plays this game incredibly humble. One thing that actually amazes me about all of our streaks is that we are a consistent winner – not consistently competitive or consistently good, which I think you can always be. To be a consistent winner in our game, I think, is a miracle because the likelihood of being consistent in this game is very low. An important part of our legacy is that we do have a consistent effort. We have an ambition to beat everyone by as wide a margin as possible, and we don't have a complacency in games that we should win easily. One of the worst ways you could treat an opponent is to assume you're better than they are. We understand that. You have to go into every game with a lot of confidence, and, obviously, we try to instill confidence in the players at every opportunity. But you start to cross a dangerous border if your team becomes overconfident. We try to demonstrate a respect for every team by playing as hard against them as we can. There's a two-fold effect. First, it helps us win as much as we do. Second, it helps us play at a very high level every single game, even games against teams not as strong as we are. Those teams get a lot of effort from us, and that improves our own game. A positive mark of our team is the seriousness with which we go after everyone. To help bring out this seriousness, we set goals within the game. Our typical ambition is to try to be one goal up in fifteen minutes, two goals up in thirty minutes and three goals up at the half. Those are our short-term goals. I think if you can break the game down and try to create the fury of intensity in those blocks of time and put teams away as quickly as you can, it takes a lot of pressure off you.

You have to be prepared from the start, so a good warmup is critical. My personal philosophy is that a pre-game warmup is a mental and physical rehearsal. It's a non-contact, technical rehearsal for what is going to happen in the game. Obviously, the warmup cannot be too intense, or you will pull the very muscles you are trying to warm up. So in a warmup period, we substitute perfection for intensity. And it's a perfection in everything, especially in their focus because you want to have a tremendous focus going into a contest. We talk about perfect passing, perfect preparation, perfect pace, perfect everything. We talk about all the elements of our warmup at the beginning of the season. We make it a very serious occasion, and we review it. I have learned over time that if you are not prepared in the warmup, there is nothing you can do in the game to recover. So the warmup for me is critical. Even where I stand is important. I like to stand right in the edge of the center circle, close to the the other team's warmup so I can assess both teams. If I can sense that their focus is greater than ours and they're doing a better job warming up, I will bring the group together. If I bring the group together, I have gotten a sense that the other team is better prepared for the match. I will say something like, "Right now your focus is so poor you are preparing to lose. If the game were to start right now, you would lose 3-0 or 4-0. You either change your mentality right now, or basically decide you are going to lose this contest."

Few people have an understanding of the dynamics of competitive team sports and pre-game motivation. They treat rankings as a pre-ordained order of finish. A soccer match is not like a swim meet where the swimmer who has the previous fastest time will win the race. Some people have little appreciation for how the lower rank itself closes the gap because motivation for an underdog is so much easier. In soccer, the capacity for a driven opponent to disrupt flow or frustrate attack is so different than a swimmer in the next lane trying to do anything to someone who is naturally faster. Many people assume peak performance and motivation are a given. They are not. It is always surprising to hear a well-wisher tell me how ready my team is going to be for a particular game. If I were rude, I would stop and say, "Why do you think we're ready?" And they would say, "Because it's an important game, of course you're ready." It doesn't matter who we are playing, or how important the game. For example, our 1987 NCAA final against UMass was one of the worst played games in history, but the semifinal against Cal was such an outstanding game, I have used it in the USSF Coaching School as a showcase for women's soccer. In many instances, the championship game in any sport pales in comparison to many "less important" games played that same season. The opponent does not automatically make you ready either. There are many subtle and not-so subtle influences that heighten and lessen motivation ... that is a book in itself. I can tell if my team is ready in the warmup, and that is the only time I can tell. No one else can tell, unless they are really studying the warmup and every player in it. It just surprises me that so few people understand what is involved in winning consistently, or in winning period. As if an event, a game, or a team automatically prepares you. It doesn't. A championship game does not prepare you for winning. A great opponent does not prepare you to be focused or competitive. The only thing that can consistently prepare you is the warmup. If things are going poorly, you have to re-organize and refocus. Obviously, some events might trigger motivation, and those are the the things you have to share in the pre-game talk. And, trust me, we always try to do our best in the pre-game talk, but the motivation has to be real. You can't invent something. The only time I can really tell how we are going to play is just before the game begins. And I am excitedly nervous anyway, even if I think we're about to tear someone in half.

Chapter 6

Having An Effect

**"If you have to yell at them from the sidelines,
you haven't coached them ... Coaching is about effect."**

There is a difference between telling somebody to do something and teaching them to do it. Telling someone to do something is what an inexperienced coach feels coaching is all about. He stands on the sideline, rants and raves, screaming: *"I can't believe it. I've told you not to clear the ball into the middle. If you don't clear it high and wide, they are going to finish that chance. How many times do I have to tell you not to clear the ball in the middle?"*

Well, there's someone who doesn't coach. If you have to yell at them from the sidelines, you haven't coached them. If you have coached something into someone, guess what, they are going to do it. Coaching is about effect. Telling someone the correct way to do something is not necessarily coaching them. There are increasingly greater numbers of people in this country that know the game of soccer. The huge number of youths from the soccer explosion in the 1970s and 1980s are now adults. But this does not automatically mean we now have huge populations that can coach the game effectively. There is a popular understanding in the coaching schools: If the coach you are evaluating is spending his practice teaching session lecturing his players with how much he knows about the game, he certainly isn't coaching them to perform. Maybe the best coaches are the ones who make the game seem simple and don't complicate practice with long-winded theories on how to play. There is also a popular theory about great players: Their natural abilities preclude them from an understanding of the process of typical player development, making them less effective coaches. To be effective coaches, they must work harder to be patient and learn the details about the process. So we all have challenges as we begin to effectively coach. The coaches with the lackluster soccer resumes need to temper their lectures and not feel they have to prove their knowledge, and the big-name personalities need to articulate their innate understanding of the game and be patient with the process.

Coaching is a lot like parenting. Parents who have produced some of the greatest kids I know, are unbelievable nags ... in a positive sense. They are always reminding their kids what to do. They are constructing a behavior for their children that will eventually become natural. By insisting that they perform this way, their children become the sort of people they want them to become. But it doesn't happen by accident. It's because there is a constant effort by the parents to instruct. Coaching and motivating players are the same way. Telling a player to get fit, for example, is not good enough. You have to instruct them about the process – how often, what kind (aerobic, anaerobic, or combinations), what intensity – so they are thoroughly educated. You use whatever you can. You nag them about it constantly because it will rarely be a natural inclination. You tease them about it if other methods don't work. Sometimes you are sarcastic, sometimes you are serious. Sometimes you bring them in one-on-one and talk about their wonderful potential and let them know the steps they need to take to reach it. You have to find their button because everyone is different. Sometimes the culture helps you do it. The culture for the women's national team is you come into training camps fit. A lot of players don't follow what the coach would like the culture to be. They follow the player's culture. They've heard the coach say, "You've got to come in fit," and they say to the other players, "He's not serious about this is he?" They hope to hear the other player say that the coach isn't serious, he says that every year and nobody ever comes in fit. But what they will hear from the players on the national team is that if they don't come in fit, they're in trouble, and in all likelihood, they will struggle. The veterans tell the new players, "You come in fit. That's all there is to it." It's not easy to establish. It takes constant effort on behalf of the coach to motivate and convince key leaders that this is what the team needs if they want to be champions. Then, through the examples of your leaders and your consistent remarks on the effects of their hard work, it develops into a positive feeling. They start to feel good about themselves. Then you support that, and tell them in front of other players who might not be fit. "You look great. I can tell you've been working hard." This way, you develop a positive feeling about all the players who work hard. Try to make that a fabric of your team, a part of your culture. If they elect to be a part of your team, they have to adopt your culture. And that, itself, becomes a tradition.

Photo by Mike Stahlschmidt

Training

Carla Overbeck:
"It was hard going against your teammates in practice like that. They're your friends, and you don't want to hurt them or hurt their feelings if you beat them."

For Carla Overbeck, then Carla Werden, the competitive atmosphere at the University of North Carolina came as somewhat of a surprise.

Despite being a very successful high school and club player, Carla did not have her pick of college soccer programs. In fact, when it came time to make a decision about college soccer, her options were to go to UNC or not play at all. She considered staying in Texas and attending one of the in-state schools and not playing soccer, but she eventually opted for Carolina.

After a week or so in Chapel Hill, she wondered what she had gotten herself into.

"I hung out with Bettina Bernardi and Tracey Bates," said Carla. "They were from Dallas too, and they kind of helped me along in my freshman year and part of my sophomore year, because I was homesick."

Soon Carla found herself in the thick of the competitive cauldron of UNC practice sessions. It took a long time for her to adjust.

"It was very difficult for me. I was always pretty fit, and I never really struggled with that. But competing, going head-to-head and kicking each other ... that was a shock to me. It was hard going against your teammates in practice like that. They're your friends, and you don't want to hurt them or hurt their feelings if you beat them. That was always hard. But it was easier knowing that everything in practice was recorded, and at the same time you don't want to see your name at the bottom of the list.

"It's funny now, but in my freshman year, I lost every single one v one game in practice. It was posted on the wall every day in the hut, and I would be at the bottom. When you see it up there, you don't want your name to be at the bottom. That definitely was a motivational factor.

"I'm not a very competitive person off the field. But it was so competitive at Carolina that I think I probably got a lot of my competitiveness there. You are going against each other all the time in practice – one v ones all the time. The players had an attitude that they weren't going to lose.

"It was not a win-at-all-costs attitude. But you knew when you stepped on the field, you weren't going to lose. If teams play like they are afraid to lose, they will."

By the way, when Carla was a senior at Carolina, she was at the top of the one v one chart. As a freshman, she never won a one v one matchup. As a senior, she never lost.

Chapter 7

It's Okay To Compete

"Women have a superior understanding that their relationships are more important than the game itself."

One of the major factors in the development of our players over the course of time is that we create a wonderful training intensity. And the toughest challenge in developing female players is getting them to compete against their friends in practice. They don't struggle competing against other teams. But when they compete against their friends in practice, there's usually a lessening of intensity.

Women have a superior understanding that their relationships are more important than the game itself. Men, obviously, never struggle with that. Men never take competing with best friends personally, but women do. I think the way in which girls are socialized exaggerates the difference between males and females. When they are growing up, girls are not encouraged to compete as much as boys. But I also think head-to-head physical confrontation with friends and teammates is not where girls are naturally comfortable. I think if you socialized a boy against competing, he would not be socialized easily, and if you socialized a girl toward competing, it would also not be easy. That is basically what we try to do here at UNC. We take young women who do not feel comfortable in those directly competitive arenas and throw them into a fierce competitive pool, and they sort of beat it into each other that it's okay to compete.

There was an interview done by one of our alumni magazines about the program, and the reporter really did a good job. This idea of competing intrigued her, and she really got to the core of this issue. She interviewed a lot of the girls on the team, and the girls told her that the difficulty they had coming in here as freshmen was that they all wanted to be a part of this great program, but they also wanted to be accepted personally. So they come into our pre-season with incredibly mixed emotions – they want to be the best they can be on the field, but they don't want to alienate anyone. They have this internal war going on between wanting to prove they are great soccer players and the social agenda of wanting to be accepted by the group they are joining. So when they go into direct confrontation with a veteran, it's almost like they feel they have to acquiesce – no matter how good they are – just because they want to be accepted by the veteran. Of course, I am standing next to them saying, "I saw you play in high school and this is not what I saw." Now, they are getting mixed messages. The freshman is getting the message from her social-ization and her gender about trying to bond with everyone, and she is getting a message from me and the girls that are beating her to death that it's okay to pound your teammates. That's the way it's done here. It's a very difficult period for them. In fact, almost every player's freshman year here is very difficult. Not just from a soccer perspective, but from a social perspective. Things they have been taught all their lives are brought into question, and it's a very difficult adjustment period. The greatest example of this in terms of teaching young women to win is Carla Overbeck. We do a lot of one v ones here. It's a direct one-on-one competition, and over the course of the season each girl plays against everyone else on the team. It's like an on-going one v one tournament among all the members on the team. In Carla's freshman year, she didn't win a game. Not one game. Her freshman year was an emotional catharsis for her because we really needed her to play, really need-ed her to win for us because she was our starting sweeperback. She was under a lot of pressure. It was a very difficult transformation for Carla to go from where she was as a freshman to what finally happened as a senior. Her senior year, she did not lose a single one v one game. By then you would not recognize her. In fact, Carla's competitive fury was so developed by the time she was a senior, she would tell me from the field, "Anson, you gotta sub So-and-So. She's killing us." She would not tolerate any lack of effort from anyone in front of her. She would scream at me to substitute any player on the field who did not give everything she had. Now for the United States National Team, she is one of the most competitive people and one of their greatest leaders. But if you saw her as a freshman, she was a really nice girl, wanting to be a part of everything. And now, if you watch her in a national team training session, she is aggressively encouraging, directing and leading every ses-sion in which she's involved. There is a competitive anger in her, and she developed it here. I know she did because I watched it happen.

If we are playing a four v four tournament in practice at UNC, and two veter-ans are on a team with two younger kids, there's going to be times when the younger kids are going to feel like easing off a bit, like it's not important. When this happens, the veterans will get on them immediately. All of a sudden, the freshmen understand that if they are not pushing at one-hundred percent, they are letting the veterans down. The veteran's body language and tone will tell them, "If you give up and we lose, I lose. That's unacceptable." Then eventually – or right away with some – intensity comes to be taken as the norm. We try to create training environments that are incredibly intense. And by recording everything, it gives the players permission to compete. It tells these women it's okay to be the best. It's okay to go after your buddy in practice. It's okay to win. And we think this competition has a hardening effect on the women on our team. A mistake many male coaches make when they are trying to make the transition from coaching men to coaching women is they try to motivate with the intensity of their own personality. In my experience, aggressive, loud, in-your-face fury does not motivate women. I know because I tried it my first few years with the team. So we substituted this "Competitive Cauldron," this "Keeping Score" to create the intense environment we knew was critical for top player development. In fact, we named one of our early clinics after it – "Keeping Score: "Training the Female Psychological Dimension." That clinic is still one of the more popular we do.

I had a long meeting with Tracy Noonan after the 1994 season. We were talking about how beneficial the season was for the goalkeepers. Rarely have we created a competitive atmosphere in goal, but we've always succeeded in creating it for field players. In 1994, for the first time in our history, we had two goalkeepers – Tracy Noonan and Shelly Finger – who we allowed to compete on the same level, even in games. During the season, we rotated who started and who played in the second half. It was all a competition to see who would play in the NCAA Tournament. So there was a competitive cauldron in goal. Tracy and I were talking about how we thought it was similar to the way Briana Scurry and Skye Eddy were developed. In 1993, Skye Eddy transferred from UMass to George Mason and took them to the national championship final, and Briana Scurry might be the best goalkeeper in the world today. How were those two wonderful keepers developed? It happened at UMass in a competitive cauldron where every practice was critical to see who would play that weekend. We discovered that the competition made Noonan and Shelly Finger each so much better. We rotated them every game. Not alternating games but basically every half. I'm convinced that's the way to develop high-caliber keepers. But it's better to have the starting job up for grabs every day. I'm convinced of that now. But I'm not convinced that you should let that keeper play the whole game. For years, I've been trying to figure out a way to develop my goalkeepers the same way my field players are developed. I know how my field players develop – there is no mercy paid on them in practice. Everything is win-lose all the time. Playing time is based on objective evaluations, and so there is a competitive fury in practice. That has never existed in goal before. What was lacking in goal? We'd go with one keeper for the majority of the season, and that would shatter the confidence of the other one. It also would not give the reserve a chance to play in games, which is critical for growth. More importantly, it would give the starter a kind of complacency, but also a kind of fear – the fear that if she ever made any mistakes, the roles would be reversed. Obviously, if the roles were reversed, the starter would become the reserve, and now her confidence is totally shattered. The reserve is now thrust into the starting position without much playing experience. Her confidence is probably not built to the extent that she really feels she can do the job. The ideal way to develop them, in my opinion, is to do exactly what we did with Noonan and Finger – split games in half but alternate who starts. Now, both goalkeepers are getting up for every game. They're competing with each other in practices. The regular season just develops them for the NCAA Tournament, but each keeper still has to compete to preserve their status. We're convinced that having a competitive cauldron in goal is the way to go. Noonan, when called upon against Notre Dame in the 1994 finals, was absolutely brilliant.

I've seen goalkeepers come to college as tremendous keepers, but end up very average. Why? They have no competition in practice. They have a complacency that stunts their growth. Coaches will try to shake things up by benching the starter after a poor performance. But the starter knows she's better than the other goalkeeper. If she didn't, she wouldn't be complacent. So good teams at the collegiate level, or at any competitive level, will benefit from having two comparable keepers, two very good keepers. And every game should be split in half. One goalkeeper doesn't win the starting job for good, which permits them to genuinely compete in practice because they know they are going to play. Save the one keeper for the do-or-die post-season tournament. Your goalkeeping will certainly benefit, as will your chemistry in goal, if handled properly. With Noonan and Finger, we told them, "We think you're very close. Both of you have earned the opportunity to play." In 1993, I made a mistake in goal. In the preseason, I thought Shelly Finger was playing better than Tracy Noonan, and I rewarded Shelly by starting her two out of every three games. Noonan was an excellent goalkeeper, but playing only one out of every three games did not permit her to feel like she was effective. The luck of the draw also gave Noonan many of the tough games, ballooning her goals-against average. When that was added to her relative lack of playing time, it did little for her confidence. In the off-season, she did a lot of work on her own, and she absolutely killed herself in the weight room, unlike any player we've ever had. Before the 1994 season, I thought Noonan was better. But Shelly was close enough to compete. I didn't want to make the same mistake again, so they split games in half. They didn't have to win the position for each game. That would be unbelievable pressure. Now you've created that competitive cauldron in practice for everyone, goalkeepers and field players.

50

Fury And Composure

Our philosophy is that the game is played with two different kinds of intensity. There's a defensive intensity, which is almost a reckless fury. In that environment, it's good to be playing completely without restraint and almost completely without composure, running around recklessly just trying to exert maximum pressure on the other team. Having that kind of mentality defensively is very valuable. However, you lose a lot of your advantage if you continue to play like that after you've won the ball. If you've won the ball, you've got to figure out a way to continue to be dynamic when the tempo is more controlled. The player with the ball has to have a certain kind of composure. Certainly in the attacking box, you have to be composed, and because finishing is such a challenge in our game, we all emphasize that kind of composure. But, in reality, any kind of ball control demands it. On offense and defense, there has to be different kinds of intensity and focus. And it's hard to bounce back and forth between playing with incredible physical recklessness defensively and then a wonderful kind of physical control offensively.

This approach has nothing to do with positional play. It has to do with possession of the ball. If we don't have possession, we all understand a forward is a defender because she's trying to win the ball back. If you've won the ball in the back, your defender is now an attacking player. This is about the different kind of temperaments required to defend and attack, regardless of what position you're playing. There's also a different psychology for each of our positions. There's no question the psychology up front is very demanding because there's constant failure, so you have to recruit the kind of athlete that has unrelenting self-confidence. You score so rarely that an attack is fraught with failure. Any successful team's front line has to have the sort of person who's so confident that she can play through failure and disappointment and still have confidence to do something positive the next time she gets the ball. The psychology used with the defender is different. There are a lot of individual rewards for any success up front, and there's very little of that in the back. But there's a lot of positive reinforcement on defense because there's so much success. The qualities required on defense are tremendous, consistent pride in your effort and a certain willingness to sacrifice your own stature for team goals. A midfielder's psychology and temperament is that of a dueler. This is the sort of person who wants to get involved in as many combative situations as possible, a person who seeks out challenge constantly. A lot of forwards can get away with resting during different parts of a game. A midfielder can't. A midfielder has to try to get involved in every part of the game. Sometimes as coaches we ignore the psychological temperament of our athletes when we scatter them around the field. It's a serious mistake.

If you scrimmaged the units against each other, the midfielders would probably win most, and the one that would lose most would be the forwards, even though they generally are the most talented. The forwards don't have a kind of consistent responsibility that a defender might have or the consistent combative presence of a true midfielder. During at least one practice each fall, we scrimmage the units against each other in a four v four tournament. There are certainly exceptions to everything: in 1995, the forwards won.

Chapter 8

The Off-Season

"For the entire off-season, all we do is play."

Over the course of four years here, a player develops dramatically. I am very proud of that. On many occasions, people have expressed to me how stunned they are at the development of our players, and unquestionably, the major part of their development occurs during the off-season. The entire fall is about developing the team to the maximum extent. All the sessions are geared toward competition and developing players in a competitive cauldron. Let's face it, the fall is still about team growth and team development. The off-season, however, is dedicated to individual growth and individual development.

For the entire off-season, all we do is play. In the fall, we're focusing on organizing the attacking box, team shape, rhythm. The fall practices are broken up into all these little pieces, trying to define and redefine our game and develop our team. The off-season isn't that way at all. It is a total contrast. We don't want the players to get bored yet we believe year-round play is crucial, and making sure each part of the year has nothing to do with any other part assures that players don't get bored. The second reason is that we want to have fun, so we just play. In a way, we are imitating what all coaches understand as the core reason a Brazilian develops into a great player. All of us in the coaching world aspire to develop players to have this incredible Brazilian touch, savvy and affection for the game. And the Brazilians developed all this outside of formal training arenas. They developed it on their own in the streets, or the beaches or on their fields. They develop just by playing. Obviously, we can't duplicate their environment perfectly, but we can try to replicate it to an extent. So we devote the whole off-season to playing whatever games we can. The ultimate game that you can play, in my opinion, is five v five – four field players and a goalkeeper. It gives you the basic elements of the game. It gives you enough players for fundamental attacking shape – penetration, width and support. The numbers also allow for classical defensive shape – pressure, cover and balance. Five v five requires consistent involvement by all the players in every attack and in every defense. You can't hide or hangout in this game, or your teammates will get shredded. It permits players a lot of time on the ball. It has every dimension, so much so that the Dutch – who on the men's side might produce the highest number of quality players per capita in the world – make a religion out of it. Five v five is an excellent compromise between the eleven v eleven game – where the ball-to-player ratio is miserable (22-to-1) and ball touches are at a minimum but has the gamut of tactical choices – and the one v one game where ball touches are frequent, the ball-to-player ratio is excellent (2-to-1) but has little tactical complexity or variety. And since we always play with goalkeepers in this environment, we are practicing finishing all the time. One more thing: It's fun to play.

We even have variety within the five v five itself. In the fall, we play intrasquad five v five tournaments three or four times throughout the season. We play with two different field dimensions: Extending the sides of the penalty box to the midstripe so the field is forty-four yards wide and sixty yards long. This five v five game has more space and requires a different kind of fitness burn than the other five v five game, which is played across the penalty box. This field goes from the side of the penalty box to the opposite sideline, so it is eighteen yards wide and fifty-nine-and-a-half yards long. Every time you change the size of the field, the technical, tactical and fitness demands change, challenging the players in a variety of ways. That philosophy carries into our off-season five v fives, where we play across the width of an Astroturf practice field with regulation goals. We also play with those old MISL indoor goals in the Tin Can (the indoor track and field facility on the UNC campus). We also play the same type of five v fives on the Carmichael Auditorium basketball court within the basketball lines using mini soccer goals, basically the same game the U.S. Indoor World Cup Team plays. Then we play one v one, two v two and soccer squash – a shooting game – all in a racquetball court. In the first game, with the large goals, there is a lot of counter-attacking, a lot of shooting, a lot of scoring. We use a regulation ball, and all we talk about here is transition and taking it to goal. The next night, we go into the Tin Can, which has a hard Astroturf surface, because underneath the turf is a cement floor. In this game, we use a different ball, a size five tennis ball and indoor soccer-sized goals defended by goalkeepers. In this game, we emphasize technical speed. One aspect of technical speed is running with the ball, and we emphasize this because there is enough space to exploit in the Tin Can. In teaching a player to have technical speed and to run with the ball, you want to have her touch on the ball be as long as possible each time. And if you try to run with this size five tennis ball under your feet, it will grab the astroturf. You have to prepare it far away from you, accelerate on to it and be as aggressive as you can with each touch. The game in the Tin Can encourages those skills because it's not like touching a size five ball, where you touch it and it bounces away. What happens is the players are given a lot of positive reinforcement with an aggressive touch, so you are able to teach players to run with it. Then we go into Carmichael Auditorium (home of the UNC basketball team before the construction of the Dean E. Smith Center) and play on the basketball court. We use a size three weighted Brazilian ball, and this ball is wonderful. This game is played within the lines of the basketball court with two goals which are used in Brazilian indoor soccer. It's still four v four, plus keepers. The size three ball is very difficult to tackle away from someone because it's so small. This ball is easy to trap and easy to control in a crowd. The emphasis in this game is solving problems technically. Now if you are surrounded by the opposition, don't just whack it out of bounds. Hold the ball and solve the problem. It's amazing how easily you can hold this ball under pressure in that environment.

One additional day a week, we go into racquetball courts and play three different games. We start out with one v one, which in my opinion is the cornerstone of the game. We set up a cone at each end of the racquetball court as goals, and now you can do anything to beat the other player. You can play it off walls or just take on the other player one v one. It's the ultimate duel. You against your opponent. No one is going to interfere. Each player plays three different games against three different opponents, and each game lasts four straight minutes. Then as a rest – because one v one is exhausting – we play soccer squash with a size five tennis ball. You're allowed one bounce and two touches to get it back to the front wall. It's basically just a shooting game. We do that for about twenty minutes, and for the last twenty minutes we play two v two on the racquetball court. We encourage the players to get in the right shape – one up high and one back – and they are encouraged to use the walls. The game is basically about combinations. You want them to pass and move, pass and move. We use a size three ball here, but now it is a regulation size three. It's a tremendous game for movement. It's also a great game for learning how to set up your opponent because, in a way, it's six against two if you count the four walls you have available to combine with. At the end of the session in the racquetball courts, we have the players shoot for twelve minutes, using a regulation ball. We vary it a bit with one-touch, first-time shots, or two-touch preparation and quick shots to get them to develop some power and a better strike.

It's important to let the players know what each game is designed to develop. Before all these games, I bring the whole group together and make one coaching point – whichever coaching point that particular game is designed to bring out. Then, I stand on the sideline and encourage that point. Obviously, I point out good things that aren't related to that one point we are working on, but I try to get the players to concentrate on the one thing that each game is designed to encourage. I don't want to cloud their brains with a thousand different pieces of information. Our off-season games are different activities which will develop a certain aspect of play. For example, on the Astroturf all we talk about is attacking and defensive transition and shooting at every opportunity because that game caters to those aspects. In the Tin Can with a size five tennis ball on a thin Astroturf field, we talk about speed of play and running with the ball. So we encourage the players to be running with the ball as much as possible. This will develop their aptitude on the run, when the ball is never static and they're always active. Then in Carmichael with the size three ball, we encourage them to never panic, solve problems technically, weave in and out of traffic with possession, and develop individual confidence with the ball in a crowd. There is nothing soccer-specific about our off-season facilities. We just took what we could find and created different games based on what was available. We made a soccer facility out of everything we could.

Before all these events, we do a Coerver warmup – changing direction with the ball and changing pace. Let's face it, the whole game is about your capacity to change speed and direction with a soccer ball. So everything in the off-season – although all we're doing is playing games – is a constant review of some aspect of the game. Each game is entirely different from the other, and you can't get burned out easily. Each one helps you become a better soccer player, but they are all entirely different. As a result, players in our program have a year-round enthusiasm for the game, which is rare. I'm not saying we can't get burned out, but we try to stay plugged into our kids. If one of my off-season captains comes up to me and says the team is burning out a little bit, then instead of playing more five v fives, we might have a one v one tournament and the next day we might have an eleven v eleven tournament to mix it up a little bit and make it more fun. And it doesn't have to be some form of soccer. At one point during the 1996 off-season, we were in Carmichael playing mini-soccer, and Nel Fettig suggested we play basketball. So after twenty-five minutes of soccer, we played twenty-five minutes of basketball.

I look at all this the same way a physical trainer views cross-training. This is cross-training for a soccer player. When you think about how Brazilians develop, they are rarely playing on the same surface. They don't always use the same size ball. They are rarely using the same kind of goal to shoot at. The shapes of their fields are ever-changing based on what is available that day, and that changes their time and space with the ball. All these things, in my opinion, have a wonderful effect on the development of soccer players. Some of the time, Brazilians are using tennis balls, which require an amazing amount of skill and agility. Sometimes they use a softer ball which is a lot easier to trap. Sometimes the goal is huge, and sometimes the goal is a can at the end of a street. But eventually, they get out on a regulation size field to play. All the different games we play are very positive for our players here because they have to make a lot of different adjustments. And it isn't easy for them. They go from one game to another, making physical and technical adjustments. And the whole time, everything is being recorded. They are winning and losing. Goals are being tabulated. It's all played with a competitive fury. And it's fun. We don't want a player to get bored. We want them to get excited about the next stage in their development.

When you think about the freedom with which Brazilians kids play, it's obvious that you have to have a certain amount of freedom to develop. I think one of the biggest mistakes we make as coaches is sometimes we straight-jacket players by over-coaching them. We have so much knowledge relative to the people we are training, we try to give them all that knowledge at once. It all relates to the coach who stands on the sideline screaming, "How many times do I have to tell you ..." If a coach ever says, "How many times do I have to tell you," what he is really saying is this: "I've been totally unable to coach you a thing, but I have been lecturing you very effectively, and I'm stunned that you are unable to take my lectures and convert them into positive soccer." You don't want to lecture to players, you want to coach them. You want to communicate information that the player takes and implements into his or her game. That's what coaching is all about. So in the off-season, the coaching points are very simple, and there are very few of them. I make them very clearly, and those are what I emphasize and reinforce when the event is going on. We don't really work on skill training in the off-season, with these exceptions: We do a Coerver warmup at the beginning of every off-season session; we shoot in the racquetball courts after our one v one, two v twos and soccer squash games, and we serve long balls. We used to do a lot of long-ball training in the regular season, but I cut that out because we ended up with a lot of muscle pulls. After the 1991 Women's World Cup when I was on my clinic circuit, I emphasized box organization and finding seams. But I also talked a lot about long-ball service and clearing. The American player is so weak at it, and our counterparts in Northern Europe are very good. The Norwegians, Swedes and Danes can all serve great long balls and can clear the ball very well. This is a weakness I wanted to correct in the American game, so we did a lot of long-ball training during the fall. We were pulling a lot of muscles with UNC and the national team when we did this, especially when we would do long-ball service after a fitness session when their legs were fatigued. I scrapped that as a consistent part of our practice in the fall and made it a part of our off-season practice when we get outdoors. There's more recovery time and less physical pressure in the off-season.

All those five v five games are a review of five weeks of our winter training. After spring break, all we really do is go outside and play forty-five straight minutes of eleven v eleven. It all gets back to the core principle of player development, which has never been very complicated: Play as often as you can and keep score in every game you play.

Chapter 9

Fit For Life

"One thing I learned very quickly
is that if you want your teams to be successful,
the players have to be responsible for their own fitness.**"**

The seeds of our philosophy about training yourself were planted before the women's national team began. It started when I was the state coach for boys in North Carolina, and it transferred over when I became the regional coach in the South for girls. One thing I learned very quickly is that if you want your teams to be successful – since you only meet them for short periods before competition – the players have to be responsible for their own fitness training. So we established very early that the players had to come in fit. We sent all of them letters with the skeleton of a fitness program that has evolved into a self-coaching program we now send to our UNC team in the early summer to prepare the varsity-eligible players for the fall.

In my experience with the state and regional team, and even in my first stint with the Sports Festival teams, I learned that it was impossible for me to get players fit in the short period of time I had them before a competition. So I developed an attitude among all the teams I trained that the players knew they had to come in fit. At first, the pre-camp fitness was on the honor system, and the novelty of the experience created a positive enthusiasm for what were obviously grueling expectations. This eventually evolved into fitness testing. I don't care how responsible your players are, if they know they have to take a fitness test on the first day of practice and they know they have to do well on it to be considered in the future, it puts a wonderful kind of pressure on everyone for performance. It also puts positive pressure on them to do some work before they get to camp. With the first couple of national teams I coached, we cut a couple of kids that didn't pass fitness. We never invited them back. It sent out a wonderful message – if you want to compete with this team, you have to take care of your fitness on your own. Also, it weeded out the kind of athlete that doesn't have a lot of self-discipline. That doesn't mean that some of these athletes never ended up competing for the United States or for the team at UNC. Tragically, there are some incredibly talented players with absolutely no discipline or work ethic. Quite frankly, they are downright lazy. But still you've created a culture of fitness for the teams you have trained, and that culture of fitness is something that has taken over the U.S. Women's National Team. At the collegiate level, it's a lot harder to develop these expectations because you have such consistent losses to graduation. Your core changes so often that you are always trying to train a critical group of players, the groups which will have the pervasive influence on the balance of the team. At UNC, it's a constant battle compared to the national team. With the national team, your core players won't leave the team that often. You know you have a group that is serious about their fitness, and it creates a very positive culture for all the people who want to be a part of the team. The new players have to adopt the training regimen that the veterans have established.

I remember when we started to promote this culture, I would speak to groups of Olympic Development Program players and coaches about the qualities needed to become a national team player. I would tell them about the six things that are required to be successful and compete for the United States. There are four general areas that we always well-understood:

1. A certain technical level
2. A certain tactical level
3. A certain fitness level
4. A certain psychological dimension

Then I would add two other areas to round out the things we looked for:

5. The kind of athlete that has the self-discipline to train on her own, the athlete who is self-motivated when there is no coach around to motivate them. This was critical, especially in a country as large as ours without an elite league in which players could develop post-college.

6. A person who is positive for team chemistry.

We wanted to establish a temperament and discipline to train hard in preparation for events way in advance. We wanted the women to adopt a Fit-For-Life style. I remember we had what the national team players now look back on affectionately as "Hell Camp." We had it here in Chapel Hill, and it was basically a fitness camp. We had it in the very early days of the national team. In this camp, we showed the players how to get fit on their own. Back in those days, I was fit enough to run with them. It was interesting, even some of our quality players didn't know how to do a fitness run. I was appalled at the great range in which people ran. A lot

58

of people ran just to survive, and they ran in their own comfort zone. If you are doing that, you are not getting fitter. In these camp runs, I would push them and challenge everyone to keep up with an aggressive pace. And many realized whatever they were doing in their own running was not fast enough. When you are dealing with elite athletes, they have to have an understanding of the demands, an understanding of what is expected of them. That's why I think it is critical to have standards. At all the levels I coached – the ODP level, the national level, the collegiate level – the standards were severe enough that in order for people to pass the testing, their training also had to be severe. The players presumed immediately that to make the team, they had to be disciplined on their own. Sure, you would love to have all the players you pick be fit, and some always will. But if they have this positive pressure hanging over their heads, a larger group will commit themselves to year-round fitness. Rest assured, when a kid goes home in the summer after leaving the University of North Carolina, they know they can't spend the rest of the summer sitting around doing nothing. If they do, they won't pass the fitness test that will be rolled out in front of them in August. It puts a positive pressure on them.

All our fitness ideas evolved with time. Originally, we just tested the players aerobically. Then we added anaerobic fitness testing after the failure, in my opinion, of our anaerobic fitness in 1991 at the first Women's World Championships in China. I was very disappointed with what was left in our legs in the final against Norway. After China, I implemented a sprint-training regimen that I got from Michelle Akers. She came into a camp a heck of a lot quicker and faster and with more explosion than she ever had before. I really liked how fast she was and how anaerobically fit she was, so I asked her what she had done. She shared with me something that she got from the Olympic Training Center about doing twenty-yard sprints, and forties, and sixties, and eighties and hundreds. Because I was so frustrated with the lack of strength in our legs in the World Cup final, I stole this stuff from Michelle, introduced it to our college kids at UNC and named it in Michelle's honor. I gave it to our kids to do in the summer before the 1992 season, and then continued it through the '92 season. If it worked for our college team, I was going to require it for our national team players. We just needed a good test first. The test was in the 1992 UNC season when we scheduled four games in four days out West. We did it as a test for what was probably the greatest collegiate team I ever coached, but also to see if this anaerobic fitness training we did in the off-season was effective. The team we scheduled on the fourth day was the second-ranked team in the country. All of our opponents on this trip were ranked teams. We played Friday and Saturday, and since our Sunday game was at a different venue, we flew in Sunday morning to play Sunday afternoon. We played the final game on Monday. On the fourth day, you would expect our legs to be shredded. We won 5-0. The scores for the whole trip were incredible. We won 5-1, 6-1, 6-0 and 5-0. In the final game, it was tied at the half, and I was thrilled about what happened in the second half. It was extraordinary how they were still sprinting and playing on the physical edge of their game. Obviously, that anaerobic experiment worked. I took it back to the U.S. Women, and we have been doing it ever since at UNC.

This concept of training on their own evolved over time, and it's continuing to evolve. For example, in the spring of 1995, we had to prepare for the graduation losses of an army of very talented and fit players. For the first time ever, we extended this philosophy to include training our players on how to stay fit year-round. And it was serious. We talk about how to maintain your anaerobic fitness by doing at least one of these anaerobic sessions per week. To maintain their aerobic base, they have to do two bouts per week, and at least one of them should be interval training, like cones or one-twenties. The other should be a hard twenty- to thirty-minute run. Not a run where they are out for recreation, but one where they feel like throwing up when they're done. We tell them, "If you are running to get fit, it shouldn't get easier the more you run. If it gets easier, you should run harder. And if you run hard enough, you should feel wasted after every run. As you get fitter, just run harder." The idea is to deepen fitness-basing, and obviously, throwing up is an exaggeration, but the point is made. In 1995, for the first time, we made it mandatory to maintain fitness on a twelve-month basis to see if we could survive the fall with a young, inexperienced team. Also for the first time, we ran two Cooper Tests. One in the fall and one in the spring. I was amazed that we had as many people pass our fitness test in the spring as we did coming into the previous season. That showed me we have educated the players on having greater personal responsibility in fitness training. Now when our season ends, they don't go into total remission like a lot of players do. When the season is over, everyone encourages players to rest. Well, the rest you should take is from soccer. That's where you are burned out. You should never rest from personal fitness training. If you have developed a deep fitness-base, the worst thing you can do is go through Yo-Yo fitness-basing, which is where you kick back, eat Bon-Bons and don't do a thing, and all of a sudden you have to get fit again. Now, you've lost the investment you've made in developing your fitness base by taking time off. Then you have a grueling fight to get fit again. Why ever do that to yourself? It doesn't take that much to maintain fitness, but it takes an excruciating amount of work to regain fitness or get fit. Our philosophy is never to get out of shape.

These fitness ideas started as an experiment by telling kids to come in and pass fitness tests. It evolved into a culture that the players have maintained and we have encouraged. We tell them, "Listen, if you want to play at the highest level, you can never lose fitness." The rationale we use is that a marathon runner doesn't win an Olympic Gold medal at age fifteen, sixteen or seventeen like a gymnast. And the reason is that fitness-basing takes time. It takes a long-term investment. Marathon runners don't go through periods of the year when they're inactive. They are always in incredible shape, and they peak for certain events. But their philosophy is to be constantly deepening their base. Our philosophy is to pour time and effort into developing a very deep anaerobic and aerobic fitness base. Soccer played at its highest level requires this, and that's what we require of these young women.

BEING HAPPY

When kids comes to college, they come with a wonderful kind of idealism, and trying to be happy is at the top of their list. They have been given their freedom for the first time. And in their ambition to become happy, the typical freshman goes out the first couple nights and gets totally wasted. They are free now, and they think a part of this wonderful freedom is to go out and stretch their limits. They think this is going to make them happy. But they discover quickly that getting drunk every night doesn't make you happy. Basically, it leaves you hung over and empty, and you really don't gain much from that kind of total freedom. There are some hilarious things that occur during those periods. But, ultimately, they don't make you happy, even if every night is filled with riotous laughter. What happens is they discover the things that genuinely satisfy them and make them happy. And the thing that makes you happy – ironically for the people who look for a quick fix – is work.

It's satisfying to work hard at something. It's satisfying to work hard at athletics. It's satisfying to compete and do your best, and those are the things that ultimately come back and give you a depth of feeling and depth of character. The process itself is not always that enjoyable, but at the end of the day, the people who have worked hard feel good about what they've accomplished. There is a satisfaction there that feeds them. There is a difference between fun and happiness. I think the most confused freshmen and sophomores we have believe happiness is stringing together a collection of fun environments. I once read that fun is something you enjoy while it is going on, but things that make you happy are what you appreciate once the event is finished. There are few environments where hard work and connecting personally are as deeply satisfying as in team sports. And if I have done my job properly, I think part of an undergraduate's evolution is they come to that conclusion before they graduate. One thing that athletics does for people is give them that satisfaction before they genuinely understand what's going on.

Player Management

Chapter 10

Leading Women Athletes

"A man's style of leadership is a very top-to-bottom structure. A woman's style is more like a network."

When we do coaching clinics and talk to people who have coached only men, we talk about the differences in coaching men and women. There is a cliché we use: "You basically have to drive men, but you can lead women." You have to drive a men's team to get them to conform to your position, but a women's team is more easily coached to that position. And, in my opinion, the way you coach women is a more civilized mode of leadership. If you read any books about leadership styles of men and women, you learn that the men's style is a hierarchical style. It is a very top-to-bottom structure. A woman's style is more like a network.

There is a great book about this called "The Female Advantage." The author, Sally Helgesen, talked about how she looked at great women leaders in the business world and philanthropy, and she took you through a typical day. The way these women led is by connecting with everyone they conceivably could within their organization. It was not by a hierarchy. A great female leader's secretary would almost be like a partner in the leadership process, and she would have a direct connection to her and almost everyone around her. No matter how far down in the organization they were, they all got the impression that they were personally connected to the leader. That is critical in coaching a women's team. All the players on the team have to feel like they have a personal connection with the coach, and it has to be unique. It seems like a male leadership style is done through status, memorandum and intimidation. The great leaders of men, the outstanding and consistently successful coaches of men, are strong personalities who lead with a powerful presence and will. Their effectiveness comes through their resolve. Yet with women, your effectiveness is through your ability to relate. They have to feel that you care about them personally or have some kind of connection with them beyond the game. Women want to experience a coach's humanity.

A coach's approach to men and women is definitely different. This, however, does not apply to young boys because I think you can coach young boys and girls the same way. I don't know if it is a hormonal thing. I don't know if when testosterone starts to kick in it makes these young boys more rebellious, but they begin to resist any sort of authority. So to lead them, you almost have to dominate them. And there are different ways to dominate them. One way is with intimidation, through the power and force of your own personality. Another one is with some sort of aggression or superior strength of ego. That is one of the things that was tiring about coaching men. This was not the case with all the men that I coached — I coached men for thirteen years. But to get them to conform to your vision of the game, there does seem to be a constant warfare between you and different personalities on your team. They all have their own opinions. You might suggest something to them, and they think, "This is not what made me an All-American in high school." Then they go off in their own direction and you have to convince them that your vision is the correct

ne. The difference between convincing men and women that your vision is correct is that women are willing to at least look at your system and try it. The men generally don't want to do anything that they are not accustomed to doing. Usually, the way you get them to try is by demanding it. To be an effective leader of a men's team you don't need a personal rapport as long as there is respect. That's the extent of the relationship. That's all that's really required. But in a women's team, respect is only part of it, and it is derived from a personal relationship. Women have to have a sense that you care for them above and beyond their soccer capabilities. If they feel their relationship with you is dependent on their soccer success, it will not be a very close and effective leadership relationship. So it's critical that women do not get a sense that there is some sort of distance personally due to some athletic failure. The personal relationship with them has to be preserved at all costs. In fact, you can destroy your leadership of a great women's team if the players feel your respect for them is based purely on athleticism or their effectiveness on the field. Women have an understanding beyond the superficiality of athletics. And what is critical to them is the way people are treated and the reasons for which you choose to respect them. Athletic prowess does not rank at the top of their list of things for which they want to gain respect. In their minds, it should be other human qualities that are above and beyond athleticism. And in reality, athleticism and soccer are not that deep and quite superficial. We all make a coaching mistake if we try to make that the priority in their lives. Your players will see through you and view you as one-dimensional.

Also, much of your coaching has to be done through a positive tone and supportive body language, even when you are upset with them and much of what you are saying is critical. Though trial and error, I have learned that the women I have coached listen less to what I say than to how I say it. In other words, they listen less to the language and more to the tone. If my tone is negative, it doesn't matter how positive the words are. They are going to hear negative. If your body language is negative, it doesn't matter how careful you are in constructing your sentences to create a positive impression. It still comes out negative. Women listen to your tone and watch your body language, regardless of what comes out of your mouth.

In Deborah Tannen's introduction to her book "You Just Don't Understand" a husband and wife are going down the highway, and the husband is driving. The wife turns to him and says, "Honey, are you thirsty? Do you want to pull over and get a drink?" And he says no and keeps driving. Well, the wife gets upset. She could care less whether he was thirsty. But it was a test of his sensitivity. He was supposed to say, "No honey, I'm not thirsty. Are you thirsty? Would you like me to pull over so you can get a drink?" And since he was just answering her question, he failed miserably. Of course, the joke is that men speak English and women speak Hidden Agenda. So the whole idea in talking to women is to understand there is a completely different conversation going on that is above and beyond the English language. And for men coaching women for the first time, the coaching vocabulary, tone and body language they brought with them from the men's game will not have the same effect. The way men communicate is by listening to what someone says and interpreting it. They are discovering in research that a woman has so many other faculties in her brain that she draws on in a conversation, and these faculties are above and beyond her intellectual interpretation of the words you are using to communicate. She is looking at your body language, and she is listening to your tone. Through a combination of all these factors, she is deciphering exactly what you are thinking about her regardless of what you are saying. It's crucial when you are coaching women to use the correct tone and body language to communicate, or at least have some sort of positive approach even if you are being critical. If you are criticizing a woman in training — and obviously sometimes you are going to — they have to get a sense that it's nothing personal. But it is hard for a male who has coached only men to do this. This is one of the challenges in the clinics I give — teaching male coaches to have a positive rapport so their relationship with the female athlete is never in jeopardy. It's difficult for men to have positive body language and use a positive tone, especially in an athletic coaching arena that is filled with frustration and correction. Invariably, what ends up being communicated is disgust. That's the nature of athletics. But when a man is criticized in this fashion, he understands it's just someone taking his game apart, not taking his life apart. A woman does not separate the two.

66

In clinics, we also talk about the use of videotape. You don't need to show a videotape to a women's team to critique them. If you are in front of a bunch of men giving them general criticisms of a game, a videotape is crucial. If you are saying there was not enough defensive pressure in the game, every male in the room is thinking, "Yeah you jackasses, I was the only one working out there. The rest of you were useless." In his mind, he immediately blames everyone else for the lack of defensive pressure. If you made that general criticism to a women's team, and said, "This is garbage. Our defensive pressure was terrible." Every woman in the room would think, "He's talking about me." So it's critical with a men's team to coach with video-tape. That way, when you make a general statement, you can look at the tape and say, "See Billy. Look, there is no pressure from your position. They are coming up their right side. You are my left midfielder, and the amount of distance you are giving that guy is about seven or eight yards." Billy will say something like, "Yeah, but he's not penetrating." And you say, "There's more to defense than stopping penetration. So what if he is not dribbling around you? You are giving him so much bloody room he can serve the ball anywhere he wants." There's a constant argument about who is failing, and you have to actually show it on tape before the guy ever has an idea that he's to blame. And even then, he'll have some kind of excuse.

So when criticizing men, it is almost essential to use videotape because they are not going to believe you. They're not going to believe they have ever made a mistake, and obviously, to a degree I'm exaggerating. But with women, a video is actually more effectively used to show that they can play well and to show the positive aspects of the performance. I think a lot of women do not have the confidence to feel they are as good as they actually are. So videotape for the sexes should be used in completely contrasting modes. Not that you can never show negative aspects of a performance to a women's team, but seeing their mistake on tape does not really help them. If you tell them they made a mistake, they'll believe you. A video almost makes it worse because they see how bad they actually were. If self-confidence is a problem to begin with, the video does nothing but magnify the mistake. Now they can see how poorly they have performed. I find it interesting that a male will look at the video and see everyone making mistakes, including himself, and start to blame everyone else for his inability. But a woman will see herself and take full responsibility for that problem emotionally. That, of course, does not build her self-confidence at all. You have to balance that with something good that she did. I do not want to pretend that men do not respond to positive things, but you have to have a balance of showing the positive and the negative. Coaches have a tendency to only stop practice during an entirely negative environment to point out and correct mistakes. Yet one of the best times to stop a training session is during or right after a brilliant series of performances to confirm exactly what you want.

Danielle Egan:
"I loved every minute I spent in this soccer program. It was one of the best things in my life."

Danielle Egan was an outstanding college soccer player. She could have gone to any school in the country, and in most of them she would have been the star. Danielle is like so many others who came through the program: Great players who were asked to blend into a great team.

Maybe she should have gone to another school? Not a chance, says Danielle.

"I loved every minute I spent in this soccer program. It was one of the best things in my life. Any young girl who wants to play soccer ... they want to come here. You gain a lot of self-confidence here. You have something that you are so good at, you can just talk about it non-stop. It comes out so easily. You can just babble on about it.

"I'm going to go over to Germany to play soccer, and I am not nervous about going to over there at all. After coming out of this program, I wouldn't be afraid to join any team."

"But the most important things I can take from this soccer program are the friendships and the relationships I've made with the players and the coaches. Most of these people are like my sisters now because I've been through so much with them. Even the ones who were seniors when I was a freshmen, I'm still really close with. And even the freshmen when I was a senior, I'm very close with. We had a close group that came in together as freshmen. There were twelve of us. Roz Santana was one of my best friends in high schools, and now we are really like sisters. We came in together and we ended together.

"I had a conversation with a friend of mine who played four years at another school, and she was saying that girls at her school come in and don't have the presence to make an impact right away. Then they start to whine about fitness or this or that. But when you come into this program, you know what you are getting into. People want to do their best and they want to win, and they want to get to the highest level they can — their own highest level.

It was just like a big family. I could be having the worst day — miserable, crying, really upset. But the girls always put you in a good mood. When you go to practice, you automatically feel better. They know you are having a bad day, and they will take extra care of you that day. I don't know any other way to say it — it's really like having a big family. We are always there for each other. Even if the person is not that close a friend, you always want to pick them up and make them feel better. Another thing is that we could always be honest with one another. That's a reason why we are so successful in this program. There's no garbage going on around here. It's that way with the girls, and it's that way with the coaches. If you need to talk to the coaches, they are there for you. They are your friends, not just your coaches. And I think that is very important to this program."

Chapter 11

Your Role With Reserves

"When you are forming any team — at any level — rarely is it filled with totally cooperative personalities."

I got this letter from Julie Carter, one of my former players. She's the one throwing water all over us in the photo on page sixty-two. Her letter shows the program from her perspective as a reserve player. I think her letter is a wonderful rendition of her positive experience here as a reserve.

Dear Anson,

It's long overdue that I write you this letter. As many times as I have thought about it, for some reason, it has been hard to put thoughts into action. I've been meaning to write you since the fall when I attended a lecture by a Dr. Benjamin Bissel called, "You Make a Difference." The lecture was focused on the administrative and clerical staff at Old Dominion, but clearly the theme was teamwork. It made me reflect on my experience at UNC and also my experiences in coaching, so far. The lecture involved a story that I wanted to share with you.

There once was a small hamlet famous for its production of grapes and wine. The hamlet was having problems administratively so they decided to elect a mayor in hopes that the situation would improve. Indeed, when the mayor came to office, his brilliance in governing the small town turned production around. Before they knew it, business was booming. The elders of the community decided that the town would reward the mayor by building an enormous vat in the middle of town, where everyone would contribute a gallon of their wine in the mayor's honor. At the end of the week, a ceremony of thanks would be held. They would pour from the spicket a glass of wine for the mayor, and he would toast to the new-found wealth of the hamlet.

Little by little, the vat was filled by the townspeople. However, one selfish villager decided that he did not want to give up his wine for the mayor. So instead of pouring his wine, he would pour a gallon of water. He would not lose out on the profit, and surely no one would notice. At the end of the week, the townspeople gathered in the center of town for the big ceremony. The glass was poured and the mayor held his glass high to the town in a toast. As he took a sip from his glass, he was startled to find that what he expected to be wine was merely a glass of water.

The moral of this story: You Make A Difference.

As I listened to the lecture, forefront in my mind was the concept of teamwork. I reflected on my four years at UNC and realized the reason we won consistently was that everyone embraced the idea that every ounce of effort each team member puts forth makes an impact on the larger whole. Even if at that moment in time, we cannot see the result or feel the impact being made, somewhere deep inside you know that you are making a difference. Satisfaction for many at UNC, including myself, would never come from seeing a reasonable result. However, it was also known to these team members or discussed along the way, that without their (my) consistent hard work and contribution, the whole team would not be carried to the next level as a unit. That is why Carolina won and wins today ... because down to the last player on the roster, it is a selfless, intrinsic effort to be the best you can possibly be. I guess there are many, many factors involved in winning consistently, but I know that one of the major factors involved in winning is team chemistry. Without it, I believe you lose the last kids on the roster. You lose their motivation to train and improve. And they do make a difference.

I've shared this story with you, Anson, because I was one of those athletes in the last couple years of my career who doubted that I made a difference. In retrospect, however, I wouldn't trade my career at UNC for anything else. I know there will be many more to sit in your office to face you with that familiar ache inside because they just can't cross the threshold to be an impact player. And you know inside — although you try to encourage them — that they probably never will. I can't imagine it being an easy task for anyone to accept a role as a reserve. But it is interesting to look back and see where I was then and where I am today. My experience at UNC has undoubtedly made me a better coach and a better person. At 18, 19 and 20 years old, I had no idea of the evolution I was experiencing. In retrospect, it's crystal clear.

So, for all those future athletes, or current ones, who sit in your office facing that hard truth, you can tell them from someone who has been there before: One can't be the best at *everything* they do. But, if you have the desire, you can always, always be the best you can be at *anything* you do. And that is all you can ask of yourself. As you experience life, undoubtedly, your personal efforts and achievements will more often than not go unnoticed by other people, but that does not take away from the importance of your accomplishments. Always celebrate your own personal moments of glory.

Thank you for being a part of my experience and my evolution. Thank you for being my friend in my career at Carolina. Thank you for the words of encouragement, for the much needed occasional hug when my heart was broken, for the tools to achieve my potential. I admire and respect you, and although we don't speak often, I think of you often. And I will not forget you.

Your friend,
Julie Carter

One thing nice about being a part of our team here at UNC is that you are a part of something greater than yourself. You are a part of a tradition of excellence. Whether or not you play a minute, you are a part of that mix. We value everyone in the program, and everyone knows they contribute.

One of the hardest things for me in my position is to make sure the reserve players are getting something out of the experience. That's very important to me because I value them as individuals and it is important for team chemistry. I want to make sure they enjoy their experience here. Obviously, someone who plays a lot is going to enjoy the program more and get more out of the experience than the ones that don't play much. Julie Carter got a lot out of it, even though she was a reserve player. It was something that she and I wrestled with because I wanted her to get positive things out of the experience, and ultimately she did. But while the process is going on, you don't realize what you are drawing from it. Julie drew a heck of a lot from it. After she graduated, she went off in a different direction, and the game brought her back. Playing soccer here was such an enjoyable time in her life, she was drawn back to consider coaching as her profession, and I have watched her work. She is very good.

Developing and balancing chemistry is a constant challenge. Establishing good team chemistry is easy if you are handed a lot of wonderful personalities. But in my experience, when you are forming any team — at any level — rarely do you have a team filled with totally cooperative personalities. Usually, if there is a division, it develops between the starters and reserves. And sometimes, no matter how hard you try or how hard some of your players might try, there is a distance between the two units. Every now and then, you can end up with an incredible bunch of reserves that fully support the starters. However, that only happens when you have extraordinary reserves, extraordinary starters or a mix of both. In the 1991 world championships, we had some examples of these types of extraordinary people who formed great team chemistry. The two best examples among the reserves were Tracey Bates and Wendy Gebauer. These two women are just phenomenal people, and they played a very important role in the 1991 World Championships. At a critical time in China, it became apparent that some of the reserve players were deserting the mission. In a players-only meeting, Tracey and Wendy spoke up and basically told everyone that we were there to win a world championship, and complaining about playing time was not going to help us at all. Their selfless attitude and some powerful leadership from people like April Heinrichs reshaped the team's unity, and the rest, of course, is history.

It's so difficult for quality athletes in any setting to fully accept a role as a reserve player. For example, any player at the national team and collegiate level is not only accustomed to starting, they are accustomed to starring. So it's very difficult for them to be objective when someone else plays ahead of them. And when a high school kid comes into college, she is used to being a superstar. Then in college, she has to fight for her playing time. It's hard for her to see that someone might be a better player. The pressure on reserve players is overwhelming, and as a coach it's not only the player you have to deal with. You are dealing with the player and her entire group of advisers. Although you are never speaking with the advisers face-to-face, and although they never see your practices, they have an opinion. Their opinion is based on what they remember the player to be like in high school or club ball. They just can't accept what is happening, even though if they were in your training environment they would see that this player is not as talented or doesn't work as hard as some of the other players. Parents just don't believe it's possible for their daughter to be outworked because they remember her as this tremendously hard worker. It's tough for them to accept that it's possible for someone to be a more effective player.

Here's a great example of the kind of person Tracey Bates is: We were playing in a tournament in Italy, and Tracey had been a starter for the national team for a year or so. All of a sudden, we brought in this kid named Kristine Lilly. Tracey and Kristine played the same position. I came downstairs from the hotel in Riva Del Garda to go running. It was late at night, about 11:00, and I was going to get a run in before I went to sleep. There was only one phone from which you could make a long-distance call, and it was under the stairway. Tracey was speaking to someone on the phone, but I didn't know who it was at the time. Well, I went outside to stretch, and while I was stretching I could hear the entire phone call. It just tore me in half. Tracey was in tears, and she was telling the person on the other end of the line that Kristine Lilly was starting, but it was a good decision. She was saying that Kristine was a great player and she deserved to start. Then I could sense the person on the other end of the line asking Tracey what she had done wrong in practice and if she was working hard enough. I heard Tracey say she was working real hard and that she had passed all the fitness tests, and, no, Anson wasn't angry with her. She was continuing to choke up over having to explain to, who I assumed was her mother, what was going on. Finally, I heard Tracey say in frustration, "Don't you understand, Kristine is better than I am."

Tracey is one of my favorite people on the face of the earth, and I was standing there listening to her try to explain to her mother that she wasn't as good as someone else. And the whole time, she was fully supporting me. She could have very easily deserted me and said, "I'm not playing because he's a jerk. He starts me for a couple of years and all of a sudden this new kid comes in and he puts me on the bench." No, she was completely loyal to me while her mother was trying to give her an opportunity to protect herself. I've never forgotten that. She didn't know I was out there listening, and she was totally committed to everything I was doing. She was loyal in a situation in

72

which very few people would ever be — not one complaint, not one excuse. After that, it's no mystery why Tracey Bates was such a critical part of the team that won the world championship in '91. But Tracey is an exceptional individual. Most people will crumble under that kind of parental scrutiny. They will blame the coach at the first opportunity and blame everyone they can think of for why they're not playing. Then they will start to believe the things they are saying, and the situation will spread and fester throughout the team. There are a lot of little things that will exacerbate the chemistry imbalance. Even the things players do unconsciously can make the team desert the mission and support their own agenda. Then you have a genuine problem on you hands. That's why I believe it's critical when you are forming a team to make sure every player understands her role and every player understands how she can play more and eventually start. This is one reason we consider these objective statistics — the ladders, the player draft (explained below) — so important. Players can basically see why they're not playing. To play more, she has to be a winner in a lot of different categories, and these qualities are evaluated with objective criteria. If a person wants to climb through the system, they have to climb through all the criteria. They have to qualify to compete.

Because team chemistry is so critical, we started instituting a player draft for the U.S. Women's National Team. I noticed at the national team level that the players who were perpetually on the bubble always felt they were treated unfairly. You could sense a genuine resentment from them over their playing time or their status on the team, and you could sense they were not taking much personal responsibility for this. It was being blamed entirely on you, the coach. I'm referring to players who come in with an agenda based on what they have been told by their group of advisers — parents, former coaches, former teammates, friends, but also friends on the team. If a girl is on the bubble, and she walks up to one of her friends and says, "Do you think I should be picked?" What is that friend going to say, "Oh no, you're awful! There's no way you are going to make this team." No one is going to say that. She is going to tell her friend that she was wonderful and she should make the team. (Although, I did overhear one girl tell another one the truth once, but then she went to someone else to get a different opinion.) The player on the bubble wants to believe that their friend is telling the truth, and they want to believe they should be on the team. But their friend is not speaking from her brain. She is speaking from her heart. She doesn't want to hurt her friend's feelings. But because the girl on the bubble is so desperate to be acknowledged, she believes it and builds her own case around it. To avoid that, we started this player draft to divide the players for competition. The statement the draft made was the true opinion of their peers as to their competitive value. The people selecting players in the draft are the team leaders. These are the ones who are most respected, most experienced and want to win — players like Michelle Akers, Carla Overbeck, Carin Gabarra, Julie Foudy, Mia Hamm, Kristine Lilly and Joy Fawcett. Usually, these were the drafters for the four v four tournaments we played at the national team camps, and we would always have a final eleven v eleven game on the last day. So you had six captains — two for the eleven v eleven game and four captains for the four v four tournament. So you got six different opinions in this draft system, and it was wonderful. All the players were drafted by their peers, and these captains know all the other girls really well. They know who quits in the middle of a game, who's going to fight to the end, who can play and who can't, who has improved and who hasn't. Sure enough, the draft almost perfectly reflected the team we selected for every tour.

Usually, the bubble players would be way down in the draft ranking. And in their exit interviews, I would be sitting there with their overall draft rank and there was no longer a question. Some players would even ask where they finished in the draft rankings, and after I told them, they would kind of nod knowingly. Now, there was less tension in the exit interview. It gets them to accept that maybe the reason they didn't make the team was something they did or didn't do. When the responsibility is on them, all of a sudden you have a great teaching environment. After you've eliminated the personal aspect of why they didn't make the team, they start listening to you and ask, "What can I do to improve?" Now, they are receptive, their hearts are open. And if they are the least bit coachable, they're going to try everything you suggest. That's a wonderful thing for team chemistry. What you want to do as a coach, as often as possible, is relate directly with the player. You want the player to trust your judgment, and sometimes it's hard for them to trust you when they don't play. Because of the organizational committee of advisers behind her — letting her know that it couldn't possibly be her fault that she is not playing — she has to feel that way. How many times do you think a girl writes a letter home saying,

"Mom, I'm just kind of lazy out there, and everyone goes right through me. I just don't work as hard as the rest of them, and I don't want to take the physical risks they do. I know you remember me from high school when I was the dominant player and the hardest worker. I'm still working at that level. But trust me, mom, there are some girls here that work even harder, and I just don't want to pay that price."

How can you tell that to your mom? It's tough to get on the phone and say things like that to your parents, former coach or friends. So their committee of advisers ends up inadvertently providing an escape clause for the player, and it is your job as a coach to get each player to accept responsibility. It's also your job to get the players to accept that they may not be as talented as other players, but if they work hard they can be a part of your system and contribute.

My all-time favorite statement made on a soccer field was at the Columbia soccer camp when I was working there one summer. We had a Parents Night where all the parents came out to watch, and there was this incredibly aggressive girl in camp. Well, this girl broke another girl's leg in front of all the parents, so everyone was afraid of her. In a scrimmage the next day, there was a fifty-fifty ball between this young savage and this sweet girl that we suspected got up early to blow dry her hair. Well, our sweet camper was just watching the ball and did not realize the savage was coming. She was cut in half. Then she got up and made the most honest statement I've ever heard on a soccer field. She said, "If you want it that badly, just tell me. This game doesn't mean that much to me." I was thinking, "Good for you!" Most players go through this pretense that they are going after the ball, and they are afraid to admit that it really doesn't mean that much to them. In a thousand different and more subtle ways, the hierarchy of your team is established through the practice and match processes that are very similar to the wonderfully honest statement that young lady made. This girl verbally shared what most girls will share physically by slowing down, timing runs so they get there just a second late, or figuring out how to get out of a tackle without taking a physical risk. Those duels and the decisions of what "means something to me" are played out constantly — ranking, qualifying and, of course, eliminating players in a continuous stream of risk, effort, focus and pain threshold. This is at the core of competitive contact athletics. The clarification of dominance is rarely so clear as this young girl made it, but it is usually clear enough so everyone on the team eventually knows where everyone stands.

The Positive Life Force

We are guilty of using all kinds of clichés, and the one we use to best describe the ideal person for team chemistry is "A Positive Life Force." Whenever I say that I always think of Tracey Bates Leone, who is the ultimate positive life force. Anyone who knows her, has played for her, with her, been around her or near her, knows what this means. I can describe her in simple terms for me. Whenever Tracy Bates would walk into my office, my day would brighten up. Whenever I would see her — even across the field — I would feel better just looking at her because she was such a positive human being with such great enthusiasm for life.

Phrases like "Good for Chemistry" don't really describe this quality. It's a force. It's a powerful life force, and she provides it. What happens is the training environment is better because she is in it, enthusiastically going after everything one-hundred percent. Regardless of the environment we were in — if there was no running water like we experienced half the time in 1991 when we were in China or the Caribbean, or when we struggled with the food in Bulgaria and China, or if we were spending the night on an airport floor — we had Tracey there. She would not complain or say a negative thing about any situation or anybody. With her, we had a positive life force, leading us by example. She lifted all of us, and my life has been better because she has been a part of it.

Chapter 12

Organizing Team Chemistry

**"In setting up positive team chemistry,
we have gone in the direction
of trying to set up a community."**

"Be a force of fortune instead of a feverish, selfish little clod of ailments and grievances complaining that the world will not devote itself to making you happy."

— George Bernard Shaw

I was raised in British colonies. I was born in India and lived in Kenya and Singapore. So I came from a different sports background. I was given an insight into the British system of athletics where you don't have starters and reserves. You have firsts and seconds. Your firsts are your starting eleven and your seconds are your second eleven. The firsts and seconds have their own schedule, so there is no one in your athletic structure who doesn't have a chance to play. Coming from this background, I got an appreciation for playing everyone in your organization. I always liked the British approach to sports. I liked that everyone who wanted to participate on the rugby teams or field hockey teams I played for got a chance to play the whole time. It was an adjustment for me coming into American athletics and seeing these selfless people who came to games with little or no prospect of playing. If their reason for joining the team was to play the game, then not having the chance was a tremendous travesty of justice. This is something that has always been a concern of mine. So from the beginning, I've been conscious of trying to form a group that is fully in support of everyone else in the group — basically organizing positive team chemistry.

We've had some teams here at UNC with great chemistry top to bottom. We've also had some challenges — and I'm talking about when I coached the men as well. I've always had tremendous empathy for the kids that didn't play, and I've always had incredible respect for the ones that didn't play yet still supported the team's mission and supported everyone in the organization. I thought that was a wonderful kind of selflessness. The example I always think of is my younger brother Pete. He came to UNC and played on the varsity for four years, but he didn't get much of a chance to start until his junior and senior year. But he was the person on the bench that was an unbelievably positive human being. There are few people I respect more than my brother for his work ethic and his positive attitude about life in general. He reflected his true character being a reserve in those situations when, obviously, he wanted to play. Since I saw Pete do this so well, in the back of my mind I've always associated the people on my bench with my brother. I've always had compassion for them, and I've wanted to maximize their experience. I don't want to sit here and pretend that every reserve player we've had here has had a wonderful experience, and I don't want to pretend for a second that any of these players would rather be sitting than playing. But we've had many over the years that have had a significant impact on the chemistry and success of our team because of how hard they worked in practice to push the starters, how gracefully they have accepted a difficult role and how honorably they have supported the team mission. They also have had an impact on the group through their personality and positive framework which they brought to the team. They have been the hidden strength of all our teams here.

Over the years, we've generally had excellent chemistry. But during the periods when I was worried for some of the people, I could never put my finger on what really contributed to everyone being close and what separated people. I believed that if I was lucky to have an incredible group of selfless individuals, team chemistry would be very good. And if we had a slew of selfish individuals, team chemistry would be bad. I thought it really came down to luck if the team chemistry was good or bad. Now I believe it really boils down to the attitudes of the reserve players and how the starters view and treat the reserves. That determines whether or not you have a genuine team.

Many years ago, I was very impressed with a Peer Evaluation program that David Allen had done with our men's lacrosse team. David works with a myriad of business organizations, and with positive peer pressure he helps build effective teams. He introduced his idea to me, and it was so good that I was tempted to use it with my team to reinforce positive team chemistry. But we were doing so well at the time, I really didn't want to change anything. I never invited him in professionally, but I kept his outline of peer evaluation. The process is an opportunity for everyone on your team to evaluate each of their teammates and share their opinion of them in a variety of different areas — attitude, work ethic and whether or not they are a positive life force. Then in 1995, we adapted his form and changed the format to a degree to suit our purposes, constructing what we felt were the critical elements of being a positive member of any team. We distributed it to the team in 1995 because in 1994 there was a division in the team that I didn't really like. Even though we had an extraordinary collection of players, there was a real division. It was not something you could see if you came out to practice, but there were two or three individuals I felt weren't really supporting the team mission. I was disappointed in that because with the exception of these two or three, I felt we had a wonderful group. I spent the entire off-season knowing full well that without everyone being on the same page, we wouldn't have the experience and talent on the '95 team to be nationally competitive. We spent a lot of time in the off-season talking about the different issues which I felt would be critical for our success. We talked about things like working harder than we ever had in the off-season, but we also talked a lot about getting together as a unit and totally supporting each other. I was very frank in my assessment of the people in the room who I didn't think were as positive as they could have been the previous fall. The first thing we did with the team in the Fall of '95 was have them do a self-evaluation on what was going to become a peer evaluation. We told them, "These are the qualities in which we want you to evaluate yourself. Later in the year, these are the same qualities your teammates are going to evaluate you in." They had a preview of all these positive qualities. They could do whatever they wanted with the feedback they got. But over time, they would all be educated as to what positive and negative qualities are, and they would discover everyone's opinion of their qualities. If they are a negative force, eventually their teammates are going to say, "Listen, you're a pain. You spend most of your life trying to come up with ways to get out of fitness. You arrange for injuries the morning of heavy fitness days, but make a miraculous recovery by game time. Under your breath, you're whining and complaining at every opportunity. I'm working so hard I'm about to pass out, and you're so negative that being near you is sapping my energy and enthusiasm. You don't make me train any harder. You haven't taken me to higher levels. You're inspiring me to, basically, cut corners. I just don't like hanging around you." I don't think these people are conscious of the way they are acting, or the destructive effect their behavior is having on everyone. If they were made aware by the people around them — who are too polite or too intimidated to let them know they are a royal pain — they would change their behavior. Nobody wants to feel they are a negative force on a team. These people who whine and complain must think they are speaking for the team or gaining in popularity by being the voice of misery. They're not, of course. No one wants to hear negative things all the time. I'm sure many of them don't understand how all their whining is affecting everyone.

In 1995, I waited to administer the peer evaluation test. I wanted to wait and give it to the team if I thought chemistry was suffering. If I felt there was a collection of people who were going off in their own direction, or several who were feeling sorry for themselves or whining, I would collect the team and have them share what they thought. Next, I thought I would tabulate all the results and bring them in individually and share what their teammates thought of them. There is nothing that makes you sit up and think more than having everyone around you tell you what you are like. I thought that would have a positive impact on behavior. After that, we would sit down and talk about it because usually your behavior starts to go off the deep end when you are in trouble, or when you start to lose, or when you're getting less playing time. I was waiting for the right time to bring this peer evaluation form out, but we didn't have a chance to use it. The reason we didn't use it was because the team was very successful, and our chemistry the entire year was very good. Over time, we are hoping this is going to be a way for us to positively affect things like work ethic, attitude, being a positive life force and whining. We are trying to construct behaviors that are demonstrations of strong and powerful character, but it will also impact on the organization as a whole. Very few players have a genuine understanding about whether or not they are positive. This will help them see.

In modern society, there is a status or prestige about being the classical American rebel or individualist. If you look at American professional athletes they always think they are not getting enough. They're not getting enough money. They're not getting enough playing time. They're not getting enough respect. It's almost like it's an endorsed behavior. And let's face it, it shouldn't be. They are not the least bit humble or selfless. For some reason, a lot of these athletes really feel like that's the way they should behave. It's like they're tough guys and no one is going to tread on them. And it does not help. When you are dealing with these athletes, a lot of them genuinely feel that this position is acceptable. They have a self-righteousness about things that have no basis in reality. This peer evaluation shows them what qualities they should have. The reason I think this has an important place in management of players is because some players don't know what good qualities people should have in team organizations. This is a way to educate them about those qualities. I have certainly tried things that didn't work. I remember one year, two players were driving me and the team nuts, so I asked them to memorize the George Bernard Shaw quote that begins this chapter. Whenever I felt they were ducking fitness or whining about anything, they had to recite the quote to the entire team. It didn't work. I don't think they understood what they were reciting. Still, it's one of my favorite quotes, and every year it finds its way onto our blackboard at least once. What follows is what I think does work. It takes an emotional investment, but like with all good relationships, it's worth the effort.

In setting up positive team chemistry, we have gone in the direction of trying to set up a team community. It's a community of people of equal value, which is almost contradictory in athletics. But I think you can create this community if the players understand that your respect for them is based on things beyond their athletic performance. With a women's team, it's critical to establish this because they are too mature to feel that athletics has any superior value. Those of us who come from men's athletics seem to feel that sports do have something intrinsically valuable. Women think that's absurd, and I certainly feel they're correct. Athletics itself does not have anything intrinsically valuable. Certainly, if you can gain a positive work ethic pursuing excellence in anything, it has value, and athletics qualifies that way. But there is nothing of overwhelming importance in athletics. There are some useful qualities that are exposed in athletic environments, things that all of us should jump on as educators, coaches and leaders. We should point to them as examples worthy of emulation. But I've never felt we should build shrines for athleticism alone. The athletic prestige is always going to take care of itself. The media and the applause will take care of it for the players. Those are not issues with which you ever have to be concerned, unless the player doesn't have any confidence. Then you can build their confidence by sharing with them how well they are playing. And building their confidence through athletics is a direct demonstration that you are concerned with them as people first and as competitors second. Women can see right through your connection with the best athlete on your team, so you have to make sure that is not your only close relationship. If your connection is based on the athletic hierarchy, you're not going to create community, you are not going to gain the respect of the reserve players and you are not going to create positive team chemistry. So we consciously try to create a community out of our team and connect with them as people first and athletes second.

I'm a fan of Scott Peck, author of "A Road Less Traveled." He also wrote, "The Different Drum" and in that book he talks a lot about creating community. It made so much sense to me because it tied into what I was trying to do as a coach. There was an early section in the book where he talked about his experiences in a Quaker school. His experiences were unbelievably positive because he felt very accepted in this school. Previously, he had gone to an elite New England prep school where the teachers prided themselves on not coddling their students. He did well in that school, but he didn't feel as comfortable as he did in the Quaker school. He said the reason he felt so comfortable in the Quaker school was that he saw how everyone was accepted for whatever they were, as opposed to the prep school where "at any given time, at least half the student body occupied the status of outcasts." I got to thinking that this is the very real problem in competitive athletics — people are evaluated and respected on the basis of their athleticism and their impact on winning and losing. They are divided first by starters and reserves, and the declaration is painful and real. You can lose your team in this division. And in the very quest for excellence, you can also divide your starters from your stars. Let's face it, in athletics, excellence can be ranked, and everyone does it. You pick all-star teams, All-Americans. You have scoring leaders. Defenses are getting shutouts. Reporters are analyzing performance. So even within your starters there are obvious divisions of excellence and appreciation. Since all these things work against community, we had to have another way to evaluate value. The point Peck makes in his book "The Different Drum" is that the kids who weren't the brightest, best looking or most sophisticated were still accepted equally at the Quaker school. I wanted to establish that here by creating a community within the team. And it isn't easy because within the team there is this hierarchy of talent and division of playing time. If you try to superimpose a different sort of connective tissue with your team, it can come across as being very phony, especially in women's athletics because they can see through superficiality. In order to establish this kind of community, you have to be genuine and connect personally with all who seek connection.

In this concept of community, everyone has a value, and respect for them is first measured by their contribution as people. Respect is tied more to their character than their athletic performance. The reserve player doesn't have to compete from an athletic standard. All she has to do is contribute from a human standard. That's the bottom line. Her value is her humanity and her character. Periodically, I share with them that there are some incredibly talented athletes that I have no respect for, and there are some very unathletic people that I think the world of. My respect for them doesn't come from their athletic talent. Other aspects are a lot more important. It also ties into the philosophy of what our mission is here. People who view the UNC program from the outside have the wrong impression of our mission. They have the feeling that this is a one-dimensional soccer factory, and they completely miss the point. If they ever came and worked our soccer camp in the summer or were a part of our team, they would sense that it is a collection of friends first and a group of people who want to compete in athletics second. When the "Dynasty" video came out, what really impressed me were the parts that Joe Patterson and Michael Sheehan, my old rugby buddies who made the tape, got from Mia Hamm, Tisha Venturini, Carla Overbeck, Kristine Lilly and Wendy Gebauer. They all said this in different ways: Soccer may have been the thing that brought them here, but it's not going to be the thing they remember. What they remember most are the friendships and relationships with their teammates. And that got me thinking — those same things are what keep me involved as well. I lost interest in soccer a long time ago. It's just not that deep. But my fascination for people, obviously, has remained. My connection with each generation has gotten better and better. When we have an alumni weekend, it reminds me just how special everyone is that has come through the program. We all feel inter-connected in a very positive way. My satisfactions go well beyond the training environment and the games. Those are reasons for us to get together and a reason for us to collectively work real hard. But the connections with the players are what make it so satisfying for me and for all the players in the program.

Obviously, as a coach you are going to have certain people — starters and reserves — with whom you are closer. I've always tried to make sure there are one or two reserves who I was close to, so there was never a feeling on the team that the only people who were close to the coaching staff were the starting players. Fortunately, we've had some phenomenal reserve players — incredible students, or just genuinely wonderful people who had an amazing interest in the team. The 1995 team was a good example. We had a young lady who tried to walk on in the off-season, named Elizabeth Marslender. Because I was so conscious of trying to organize a new team and because I was so concerned with chemistry, I didn't let her join the team in the Spring of '95. Well, it was a huge mistake. In the fall of '95, we were so down in numbers, we were recruiting the campus to find people to fill out our roster just so we could scrimmage. Someone mentioned Elizabeth, and I said, "Sure, have her come out." Robin Confer brought in another player named Erin Bialas. She played with Robin in high school and was the class valedictorian. They were pure walk ons, but sure enough, Elizabeth and Erin contributed significantly to team chemistry. In fact, they were such amazing people and so wonderful for the team, I spent one pre-game talking about them because they made a significant impact on all of us. I trusted them so much, I even turned over my recruiting weekend to them. As history will bear out, the 1996 freshman class is one of the best we've ever had. Erin and Elizabeth are the type of kids that genuinely wanted us to do well and cared about the entire group. This kind of respect for the reserve player and the respect from the reserves back to the starters and to the whole team is critical for establishing this kind of community. They could sense they were respected and were a part of the organization. Even though the playing time wasn't doled out to them in equal portions, they could sense they were a part of the team and all of us liked them, and in fact, they were valuable. This concept of community is something we've been conscious of for a long time.

We also try to involve the parents as much as we can. This made a positive impression on everyone on the team. The parents who are able to come to the games act as sort of surrogate parents for all the players. The tradition has established itself now so that the collection of parents we have in the pre-season, major games and NCAA Tournament games is phenomenal. We make them a part of everything we are doing, and it's just a wonderful kind of atmosphere which has a positive impact on establishing us as a community. We demonstrate to the parents that we value their daughters regardless of where they stand in the team-talent hierarchy. We value them as people. This sense of community which is very difficult to establish is in place now, and it is a tradition that helps contribute to our success as an overall organization. We will always do whatever we can to keep it.

Self Evaluation/Peer Evaluation

" Positive impact for change is brought about by peer pressure rather than management pressure. Self-development is encouraged by providing players frequent, accurate, confidential information from their peers so they can grow and develop. "

Instructions

- Appraise each team member's DISCIPLINE, ATTITUDE, PERFORMANCE AND CHARACTER.
- If you appraise less than "A," please write ONLY ONE improvement code.
- Rate yourself

Descriptions

A.   Excellent Performance
B.   Good Performance, but could use a little improvement
C.   Fair Performance, but definitely needs improvement
D.   Poor Performance, with serious problem areas.

Adapted from David Allen's PEER PLUS — Communication and Motivation Resources for Organizations to Improve Attitudes, Quality and Productivity

Self Evaluation/Peer Evaluation Form

Discipline

1. **Fitness-Basing:** Has the understanding to maintain and, when necessary, deepen fitness-basing through aerobic, anaerobic or interval work on year-round basis.
2. **Skill Development:** Has the ambition to become the best player possible by improving on weaknesses and building upon strengths.
3. **One v One:** Has the psychological strength and desire to play one v one even when it is not required because this is the cornerstone of our game.
4. **Weight-Training:** Has the discipline to lift on a year-round basis because it protects you from injury and maximizes your athletic potential.
5. **Nutrition:** Has the understanding and discipline to know what, when and how much to eat and drink.

Attitude

6. **Teammates:** Being friendly, helpful, responsive and caring to teammates.
7. **Coaches:** Respecting and supporting coaching decisions and directions.
8. **Professors:** Respecting and cooperating with professors.
9. **Program:** Contributing to the reputation and growth of the soccer program.
10. **Self-Development:** Showing the desire to take specific steps to improve as a player.

Performance

11. **Academics:** Hundred-percent effort in attending classes and study hall and using available resources — library, etc.
12. **Practice:** Always intense in practice; training on your technical and physical edge.
13. **Competing:** Always playing to win, feeling you are the margin of victory, never giving up.
14. **Community:** Being non-judgmental and supportive of everyone in the program.

Character

15. **Mental Toughness:** Staying focused, doesn't get down on herself, teammates or coaches.
16. **Reliability:** Making curfews, coming to practice, meetings, games on time.
17. **Confidence:** Having faith in her abilities without being conceited or arrogant.
18. **Commitment:** Promising to do her best, maintaining personal integrity.
19. **Conduct:** Displaying behavior consistent with program philosophy and moral principles.
20. **Positive Life Force:** Always supporting teammates behind their backs to build a positive system and community where everyone is valued in our team organization.

CONFIDENTIAL

Women's Soccer
University of North Carolina

	Attitude		Performance		Character		Discipline	
	Letter	Improv Code	Letter	Improv Code	Letter	Improv Code	Letter	Improv Code
Erin Bialas								
Robyn Brallier								
Robin Confer								
Sarah Dacey								
Aubrey Falk								
Nel Fettig								
Leslie Hutton								
Rye Johnson								
Rakel Karvelsson								
Debbie Keller								
Amy Lincoln								
Elizabeth Marslander								
Siri Mullinix								
Tracy Noonan								
Cindy Parlow								
Ashley Riggs								
Amy Roberts								
Tiffany Roberts								
Vanessa Rubio								
Beth Sheppard								
Amy Steelman								
Sonja Trojak								
Meg Uritus								
Staci Wilson								

Chapter 13

Protecting The Take-On Artist

**"If you have a take-on artist on your team,
it's your job as a coach to preserve that creative quality."**

We have a rule: "If you have one player to beat to either shoot or cross, you have to beat that player." There's only one excuse for not beating the player in that situation: If your pass results in a first-time shot on goal from a better angle.

As a result, all of our players feel secure taking on. They know it's part of the system, and they also know it's not always going to work. And that's okay. In fact, they hear criticism more if they successfully pass when they should have taken on, than if they are stripped in the one v one attempt. Some of them are take-on artists when they get here — obviously, because we recruited them for that very quality. If we see a creative one v one artist out there, we go after them. We write letters to these players when we're recruiting them telling them, "Listen, if you like to take players on, this is Take-on Heaven. You come to the University of North Carolina and you are following in a long line of dribbling phenoms. Our system is designed for you." And it truly is. Our system is designed for these types of players to get better. We encourage it, and we never reprimand them.

My first recruit, Janet Rayfield, who came to play for me in the fall of 1979, liked to beat players. So did Stephanie Zeh, who came in 1981, as did Joan Dunlap and April Heinrichs in 1983, Carrie Serwetnyk in 1984, Wendy Gebauer and Birthe Hegstad in 1985, Rita Tower, Kristine Lilly and Mia Hamm in 1989; Danielle Egan in 1991, and more recently Robin Confer in 1994 and Cindy Parlow in 1995. These were women we played up front or on the flanks, and we tried to isolate them as much as possible to set up their one v one duel. Since their first instinct was to beat an opponent whenever they had the chance instead of play-make, many of them started playing soccer without what overly critical people would consider the "team-oriented" attacking package.

Every now and then, these personalities would take players on in situations where they shouldn't, or they would shoot from impossible angles. But you have to be careful in making any kind of critical instruction because you don't want them to lose their wonderfully reckless desire, the one v one mentality to do it all on their own. Periodically we suggest things like this, "You know that time you were taking on those six players, well, that teammate on your right was totally unmarked. And in that environment, obviously, it's going to be better for us if you find her." But this is always a gentle suggestion. If you have a natural take-on artist, it's your job as a coach to preserve that creative quality and nurture the psychological traits that cause her to constantly do that. A lot of fans, parents and some coaches will talk about selfish players, and you discover that they don't know what they're talking about.

I remember when I went to recruit Stephanie Zeh. She is one of the greatest players I've ever coached, but her career was cut short because she had her ACL cut in half in an NCAA semifinal game against Central Florida. When we went to recruit her, all the parents knew that North Carolina was coming up to scout Stephanie Zeh. I'm on the sidelines walking through all these parents, and all of them are telling me the same thing, "Coach, I don't know if you want her. She's not a team player. She just dribbles the ball." The more I heard this, the more excited I got. I initially went up there with a small scholarship offer. By the time all the parents had told me I didn't want her, I was considering giving her a full ride. She had angered so many people because she took players on constantly. Imagine the strength this seventeen-year-old girl had to have to keep taking people on when everyone hated her for doing it. Imagine the strength this young girl had to have to maintain the confidence and soccer arrogance to keep dribbling in the midst of all this unbelievable criticism from her teammates and all their parents, and probably coaches, too. She had to be unbelievably powerful if I'm standing on the sideline and the parents are telling me not to recruit her. I'm thinking this girl has got to be a psychological rock to thrive in this environment. Can you imagine the number of girls that don't have that kind of strength, but have Stephanie's talent? They could become wonderful take-on artists, but under the barrage of constant criticism — "You're not a team player; you won't pass to my daughter; why don't you pass to me; you're incredibly selfish" — they finally collapse and become these passing players who are a dime a dozen. Sometimes, in their desire to create wonderful human beings and unselfish children, parents sacrifice the quality that makes soccer players great. Yes, I think it's wonderful that their daughter's a team player and bends over backwards for everyone and is real sweet and cooperative and is always looking to pass before shooting. I'm sure she's a real sweet girl. But that girl's not going to help me win championships. It doesn't mean that she's not going to have a place on the team and contribute to team success. But Stephanie Zeh, Mia Hamm, Kristine Lilly April Heinrichs, Michelle Akers, Carin Gabarra, and those great

87

midfielders who can take on in order to pass, like Emily Pickering, Marcia McDermott, Shannon Higgins and Tisha Venturini — those are the ones that win championships for you.

You have to let these players know what kind of freedom they will have. Tell them, "In my system you are my personality player. You have the freedom to do whatever you want in this game. So if you want to take players on in your own penalty box, go ahead because that's the kind of freedom I'm going to give you." And I've given players that kind of freedom before — April Heinrichs, Shannon Higgins, Kristine Lilly, Mia Hamm and Tisha Venturini at North Carolina, and Carin Gabarra and Michelle Akers on the national team. These are players that you don't restrict. You don't tell Carin Gabarra that when she's on the mid-stripe it's a play-making zone and she shouldn't take players on in that zone. You should be able to tell her that looking up and serving the ball might be more effective. But you never tell her that's the way she has to play. You suggest that play-making is what should be done in this zone, but make sure she knows she is your personality player and when she gets the ball in that zone, she can do whatever she likes. Then you start to get the goals she got against Germany in the 1991 World Championships, where she wins the ball within ten yards of her own mid-stripe, does what she wants, looks up and hits one from thirty-five yards in the upper left corner of the German net. That's one of the greatest goals I've ever seen in competition. If she had to play-make in the middle third of the field, she would have knocked it up to someone else, and all of a sudden that goal wouldn't exist. You have general guidelines of decision-making in general thirds of the field. But then with your personality players, you say, "This is a guideline, but as far as I'm concerned, you make any decision you want." You have to be careful, though. You have to protect her from her teammates. They are going to be jealous because they're going to be unmarked on the six-yard line, and one of your personality players are going to be near the endline with no shooting angle, and they are going to shoot. You protect her by telling the teammate, "She should have found you, but still I don't want to lose the quality that got her to the endline in the first place. If I start berating her, we're going to lose that quality. You don't want to lose that quality in her do you? No? Well, neither do I." So you protect her. You let the player standing alone on the six know that the best choice would have been to pass it to her. But if the best choice had always been for this player to pass it, she wouldn't be the player she is.

When they came to UNC as freshmen, Mia Hamm and April Heinrichs were two players without service as a natural part of their games. To show how much they developed, look at Mia's stats as a junior, they were unbelievable. She had thirty-two goals and thirty-three assists. Thirty-three assists! That's mind-boggling. That's because she developed this take-on ability on her own. All of her coaches all of her life, basically, protected it — or maybe they didn't, but Mia was so strong that she basically did what she wanted anyway. At UNC, we weren't about to tamper with her remarkable creativity. We protected that quality as best we could, but we also told her about her options, better shooting angles, knocking it to a teammate for a one-touch shot. You review the options, not berate her. She could do the hardest things first. I was never worried about the rest of her growth. Then she comes into her junior year, and she's doing it all. She's beating the players at the right time, scoring on her own, and when she's trapped or surrounded or they're stacked up on her, she's finding players in seams. Her game is remarkable. The same with April. Her first couple of years, she felt more comfortable penetrating on the dribble than serving it forward or playmaking. That was fine with me. And like no freshman I have ever seen, April did not let the fact that she was a first-year player interfere with her desire to win first, at the possible sacrifice of that year's Miss Congeniality Award. She destroyed people in practice, she destroyed teams in games. Whenever she got the ball in the game, she would go through the whole defense and score on her own. We'd give her the ball, and I would tell everyone else to get out of the way because there's no reason to take defenders anywhere near her. April could beat the whole team without help most of the time. All we had to do was look for a rebound. And then she started to learn the system. In her junior year ... same thing as Mia. She set a personal assist record. By then, she was expanding her game and starting to assist as much as she was scoring. But like Mia, the base of her game was overwhelming. And when you are fortunate enough to be handed this kind of talent, you don't want to get in its way.

The Dueler

For a long time, we have been trying to refine our competitive arenas. We are constantly looking for new ways to compete, and we are always trying to improve the ones we have. We have a pretty good idea of a fundamental group of things in which to compete. There is a core of things that we started from the beginning that we haven't changed, like the one v one, which is incredibly important for us. We have made additions to the one v one, but that personal duel is a cornerstone of our success.

I remember when I went to my first USSF coaching school in my early twenties. The instructor said the team that wins the majority of the individual duels in a game, will win the majority of the games. So the foundation for your success in a game will be how many individual duels your players win. Duels are beating players or stopping players in one v one situations — winning head balls, stepping through on a fifty-fifty ball for possession. Those duels are critical, and the team that wins the majority of those duels will win the majority of the games. As a young coach, that was my foundation — to teach my players to be duelers. That's still a part of my coaching personality. It was taught to me in the Federation schools, and I was sold on it from the beginning. I still think it is a fundamental part of soccer success.

Tactics

Chapter 14

The Value Of The Three Front

"With a three front, you are going
to have a chance to beat teams that you would normally tie
and upset teams you would normally lose to.**"**

What I've been convinced of from the beginning is that there are a lot of differences between the women's game and the men's game. When I was originally asked to speak on these issues, it was at an NSCAA Convention back when I was just beginning the UNC women's team in the early 80s. It was the first real clinic given on the women's game at the NSCAA convention, and it was poorly attended. There was a core of women's soccer fanatics on hand, the few of us that were involved in the game. I tried to share with these people my experiences in the difference between training men and women. In those days, I really didn't go into much detail on the psychological difference, because I was just beginning to formulate my opinions. But even way back then, I was trying to sell people on playing a three-front in the women's game.

I'm convinced that a part of our success at the University of North Carolina and a lot of our success in the international arena is because we separate the two games — the men's game and the women's game — tactically to a certain extent. Because a lot of the top coaches in women's soccer come directly from the men's game, all of them have a comfort zone and a direct attachment to the men's game. I remember when I first started talking about training women, I always compared it to training men because my original experiences were with men. It was very controversial, and even to this day it has a lot of controversial elements. Many people, in an effort to try to be politically correct, try to minimize the difference between the men's and women's game. When people speak on women's soccer, they try to say that it's just soccer. And when they train female goalkeepers, they say they are just

92

training goalkeepers who might be a little shorter and have less of a vertical jump. They are all paying homage to some sort of historical judgment, which in my opinion, reeks with a kind of weakness that people flock toward when they feel political correctness is more wholesome than the truth. I've never been afraid to separate the two, and I think that has always been a great advantage.

The big advantage of playing a three-front is that almost every other team plays a two-front. Every time a team plays you, they have to adjust. Every time a team plays the University of North Carolina, they are adjusting because they are accustomed to playing against a two-front. Now they are thrown in against a three-front, and it takes them out of their rhythm in terms of play-making out of the back. When they try to come out of the back, they are dealing with an extra player pressuring them, and they have to re-organized themselves defensively. I've always thought it gives us a wonderful advantage. When Duke beat us in 1994, their coach, Bill Hempen, was a very humble winner. He said something in the press that I really appreciated. He said one of the reasons he beat us is because he learned from us. One of the things he learned from discussions with me about team organization is that with the three-front you are going to have a chance to win more games. You are going to be less prone to be upset than you would if you are playing a two-front. Another advantage of the three-front is that you are going to have a chance to beat teams that you would normally tie and upset teams that you would normally lose to. Well, Duke played a three-front against us. And against a three-front, we are going to have to make an adjustment because we rarely see it. We are not as comfortable playing against it. If the other team is playing with three front-runners, we have a more difficult time getting out of the back. We are going to have more people who are responsible for marking or covering a zone if the other team is playing a three-front. They are going to have more players in the attacking box. Those are facts. When Notre Dame beat us in the 1995 NCAA semifinals, they were in a three front.

The key to consistent victory is getting numbers in the attacking box, and it's all related to women's ability to cover the field effectively. The ultimate advantage, in my opinion, is that the three-front covers the field better in the women's game. I think most of us as coaches have a tendency to be conservative, and the men's game basically goes in that direction. It's a more conservative game. The media pressure of the men's game is so high at the levels we emulate — at the World Cup level, First Division teams in Europe and South America. Coaches' entire lives are based on their success. The easiest way for them to prevent getting fired isn't so much to be overwhelmingly successful, as to not be humiliated or embarrassed. So they don't take as many risks. As a result, most of their teams play a very conservative style. They put more players in the back and crowd the midfield, hoping to steal a goal with some great individual effort or a lightning run out of the back. That's not going to work as well in the women's game. Take a woman relative to a man in terms of her speed, quickness and ability to change directions. A woman is not as fast and not as quick as a man. But she is basically playing on a man's field. Think if you put a man on a field that would have a similar ratio. Figure out the basic difference in speed between a man and a woman, which will give you the basic difference in her ability to cover the same amount of space. If we asked a man to play on a field the size that women are asked to play on, the man's field would probably be about one-hundred and thirty-two yards long and about eighty yards wide. If you asked a male player to play in a 4-4-2 on a field that size, then asked those flank midfielders to get in the attacking box every single time you had a successful attack, their lungs would be exploding in their chest. It's physically impossible to make those demands on male players with this larger field. Not that they wouldn't occasionally get into the box. They would, just like in the women's game. The idea is to get there every time you get the ball up there. With the three-front, you are already starting with one more player forward, so the odds of consistently getting one more player in the box are going to be better than they would in any other system. The other problem that we present in the women's game for those unfortunate two players up front is now they have an enormous amount of space to track if they want to put any kind of pressure on the opposition. Again, it's like asking two men on a field eighty yards wide to not let the four defenders come out of the back. They would have to track from sideline to sideline, and they would be exhausted. They will not be as effective as attacking players if they are asked to cover that kind of space defensively.

I would venture to say that almost every national team forward I have trained who has come from a two-front environment, loves it when they come into our system. Not that we don't ask our forwards to do a lot of work. We do. We put incredible demands on our forwards, both offensively and defensively. But they don't feel the situation is as hopeless offensively or defensively when they are playing with three up front. I have yet to get a forward at any level that hasn't been excited about our system. I'm talking about the best — from a Michelle Akers and a Carin Gabarra, who came from two-front environments, to players we recruited out of two-fronts that came here to UNC. In fact, when we are recruiting front-runners we show them the legacy of our success in terms of goal-scoring, but also talk about the dynamics of our front line. We tell them, "You are going to play in a system that attacks at all costs. We have a history of forwards that have gotten spectacular results, players that really enjoy playing in a system that is committed to going forward, committed to them." The 1994 season is a wonderful example. We had a very young and inexperienced forward line, and we thought we weren't going to score many goals. I thought that if we were going to be successful, it would be because we would be very well organized on defense, and it would be very difficult to get through our veteran midfield. I thought we would win games against the best teams 1-0. The irony is that we scored more goals that year than we did the year before when we had Mia Hamm, one of the greatest forwards of all time. It's a tribute to a wonderful senior class that was in place, but also it's a credit to a system that encouraged players to get forward and score goals. We ended up scoring goals in buckets.

There is another mistake I think we make with the women's game. Because most of the women's coaches started out coaching in the men's game, we take the current evolution of the men's game and immediately put it into the women's game. But our game hasn't evolved to the same level as the men's game. Obviously, we have made great strides in the women's game, and it is becoming a better and better overall game. Still, the men's game is technically sharper and tactically quicker. I think we have elements of our game that are very attractive and great to watch, but I am not going to say we have caught up with the men's game. If you look at the evolution of the women's game, maybe we have evolved to the point when men were still playing a three-front. Maybe that's where the women's game is in terms of our soccer evolution. And maybe before we get to the next level, we need to evolve further in an older system. Perhaps, a lot of coaches are making the assumption that both games have evolved to the same level. They haven't. The men's game is still technically cleaner and tactically faster. And because the women's game is not yet technically and tactically efficient coming out of the back, all of us would benefit by high-pressuring teams early with a third front-runner. Not only will your team win more balls in the attacking half, you will also force the other team to play faster than they are accustomed, causing frantic, inaccurate passes that your own midfield or defense can pounce on.

Without three front-runners, it would not be possible for us to have the same kind of box organization that we have now, and a lot of our offense depends on it. We would have box organization, but not to the same extent. For example, we can't frame the goal as well with fewer numbers. A lot of our box ideas were stolen from teams that play a two-front. But because we throw in that third striker, it magnifies the effectiveness of what the men are trying to do with two. What impresses me about many of the teams we face internationally is how efficient they are at finishing with just one other player in the box. They have one player who gets forward with the ball and one other player in the box to finish. But they are efficient at it. In the men's game, I'm always stunned to see one guy get to the endline, drive the ball across, and in the midst of four defenders, find his attacking mate. It's almost a technical and tactical development borne out of necessity. That is where the men's game is right now. I don't think the women's game is there yet. We don't have the precision on our crossing, and we don't finish as well with our heads. In fact, we have other problems defensively that should further encourage the third front-runner. Our defensive boxes are very vulnerable to poor clearances, so there is another wonderful advantage in having a third player already posted forward to finish anything miss-cleared in and around the defensive box.

Chapter 15

Field Organization

"We have put a concerted emphasis on finishing our chances, and it pays off for us year-in, year out."

There is nothing profound about our attacking philosophy: We try to get the ball forward as quickly as possible and take the attacking space we are given. If the opponent is flat or if we can organize a run through the restraining line, we play behind the defense. If the defense is deep or the pressure is too great to penetrate directly, we serve the ball to the strikers who are withdrawing, and we play in front of the defense. We flood zones up top, so if the ball is on the left side of midfield, all three forwards are making runs on that side of the field. Ultimately, we want to get into the opponent's penalty box quickly, and we try to get there in numbers.

Defensively, we play a combination man-to-man and zone. Based on whether the opponent is playing a three-front or a two-front, we match up accordingly. Against a two-front, we mark man-to-man against their front-runners, sweep with one player and play a pressure, cover, balance, high-pressure zone up top with three front-runners and four midfielders. If we see a three-front, we throw in another marking back, eliminate a midfielder and play with three forwards, three midfielders and four defenders. The front six are still in an active pressure, cover, balance zone, and we are still marking in the back with a free sweeper. We try to pressure early up front and swarm the ball in the midfield and in the back by having the front-runners double-back against the ball in the midfield, the midfielders double-back against the defense with the sweeper doubling forward. Both our attack and defense require extraordinary amounts of running, so during seasons when we have great depth, we rotate five players up top and six in the midfield. We have even rotated markers on occasion to keep a relentless pressure on quality front-runners we face.

Our philosophy is to play high-pressure defense from the beginning of the game to the end and challenge our opponent to fight through four combative lines of defense to get to our goal — our forward line, midfield line, back line and our goal line protected by our goalkeeper. We put pressure on an opponent as early as possible and try to keep that pressure up for ninety minutes. We feel that if a team can hang with us and equal our intensity level for ninety minutes and score goals, they deserve to win, period. Our attack is designed to get players forward in numbers and every player is encouraged to get involved These are the things we do to play against the opponent. But you also have to play against the game. Playing against the game is the incredible dichotomy of how difficult it is to score and how easy it is at the same time. We have all been part of this example: You completely dominate a game, outshoot an opponent by a wide margin and end up losing. So when playing against the game, you've got to figure out a way to finish the chances you create. And that's not an easy task, even against a team that is not as good as yours. We have a concerted emphasis on finishing our chances, and it pays off for us year-in, year-out. A lot of the clinics I have given over the years are on box organization. And within box organization, comes framing the goal. Framing the goal is a very simple idea that everyone in the country understands but very few coach. It's the idea that whenever a player takes a shot, you have a player running at one post, another one running at the other post and another running at the goalkeeper ... assuming you have the luxury of having that many people in the attacking box. But we try to arrange to have that many people in the attacking box, and the reason we can arrange it is that we play with three forwards. If someone is taking a shot, we try to have at least three players forward in the attacking box to frame the goal properly. And we work on this constantly.

In the midst of all this, we work on finding seams in the box, which is a method of trying to organize chaos. The goalmouth is chaotic with all the bodies in there and everyone running around creating havoc. We try to get our players in environments to find finishing seams. If you have beaten the defense to the endline, one finishing seam is the space between the goalkeeper and the defender you have just beaten. This seam is that untracked line where the ball can be played by an attacking player to be finished. Other seams can be found between any two defenders in the box, where an attacking player can appear and either finish the chance, or begin a seam-finding, play-making ritual again, but now it is from a more dangerous position within the opponent's penalty box. What makes the service of these seams so dangerous is that even in what is a cluttered box, you are playing the ball low or on the ground into a channel where the defenders are not. And the tactical instructions and concepts are very simple: The server must find the seam by simply not hitting a defender with the ball. The finisher or play-maker must be there when the ball is there. So we are trying to elevate our team from just mindlessly whacking the ball high into the box and hoping to hit a teammate. Mindfully avoiding defenders and keeping it low provides less time for the defense to react and organize. Sometimes there are no seams, and the box is too crowded to do anything but flight the ball, hopefully, behind the last defender and out of reach of the goalkeeper. In the classical endline series of near-post, far-post and slot runs, the bending flighted ball to the back post still has the highest finishing percentage, but this does not mean you eliminate the other runs. The choreographed runs at the slot and near post are still critical because they cover your margins of service error. The extra numbers in the box also help you frame the goal effectively. If the near-post player sees the ball go over her head, she can frame the goal by turning around and making sure that if the ball is shot wide near her, she can close that shot and finish it. And the player who's making a run to the slot (the center of the goal near the 12-yard spot) should continue her run at the goalkeeper. That way, if the back-post player hits it and the goalkeeper drops it, this slot-runner finishes it.

We don't assign certain players in certain positions to run to this spot or that spot. It's all based on the run of play. It's every player's responsibility to organize the box, but what we do is call on the personality players — the vocal ones — to take charge. The closest player to the near post has to make the near-post run. The closest player to the far post has to make the far-post run. The closest player to the slot has to make a slot run. Generally, the center forward is making the near-post run. Generally, the center half or attacking midfielders are making the slot run, and the left wing or left half is making the back-post run (assuming the ball is being served from the right side.) You guard against becoming predictable by letting the flow of play determine who makes the runs. They can decide for themselves where they have to be. Every time the ball or a player moves, angles change. And when angles change, decisions change. Even though there is some choreography involved in box organization, it is done off the flow of play. All the runs are somewhat different based on where the defenders are, where the ball is, and where the ball is going.

Even in the midst of every set piece we run are the concepts of framing and organizing the box effectively. Our corner kick is a model of framing the goal. At the near post, we have a player get in front of the other team's zone, which is what Sarah Dacey did in the 1994 finals against Notre Dame. A flick past the zone nullifies the effectiveness of the zone. We have a player running at the back post, like Angela Kelly did against Notre Dame, to finish any ball that ends up there. We had Tisha Venturini running down the middle in the event the ball is there. Once the ball goes over Sarah's head, she turns around to frame the goal on that side. So if Tish were to end up with it, Angie and Sarah are framing the goal on each post — just like Aubrey Falk did in the first goal against Connecticut in the 1994 semifinals. On that goal, Nel Fettig received a short corner at the near post, served it to the back post to Angie, who didn't have a finishing angle. Angie headed it across the face of the goal and Aubrey Falk was framing the goal on the other side and put it in. What was neat about it was, Jerry Smith, the Santa Clara coach, was sitting in the stands next to Tony DiCicco watching us score these goals against Connecticut. He turned to Tony and said, "Anson coaches that, doesn't he?" And Tony said, "Absolutely." We do box organization constantly. We spend a lot of time organizing the attacking box, and we try to organize all aspects of it. We talk about this in the pre-game. We tell the players that the way we organize both boxes will determine whether or not we win. So even though all I have addressed here is offense, we don't just organize the attacking box, we organize the defensive box as well. To train both sides of box organization, we do a practice series called "Team Trains the Keeper." We have a group of players in a half-arc around the goal, about thirty yards out, serving balls into a goalkeeper. There are two defenders with three attacking players on them. We have the attacking players front the defenders and make sure they're not a part of a clearance. We have three players on the top of the "D." They alternate finishing after the ball is cleared. While the shots are being taken, two of the players frame the goal on either post, basically, making the goal wider. The other player attacks the goalkeeper. So what's happening here is really attacking-box organization. But what's also happening is that the goalkeeper is playing the ball. As soon as these attacking players in the box can see the girl shooting, they clear a little room to expose the goal. But they also must be in a position where if the ball is about to go wide, they can re-direct it. They're actually putting a funnel on the goal. So they're making an eight-yard wide goal twelve yards wide. The defenders are active as well. If the keeper steps out to challenge the shooter, they drop into the goal behind her to clear balls off the line. The environment is basically a frenzied box, and it replicates the scramble that takes place regularly in both boxes every game.

One of the interesting challenges about women's soccer is you're playing with a ball designed for men to shoot and catch. It's harder for women's hands to catch this ball because they aren't as big as a man's hands. In the women's game, the goalkeeper parries the ball a lot. When she parries it, our girls are in these areas waiting. Or if she tries to catch it and can't hang on to it, she ends up dropping it where our players are waiting to finish. We spend a lot of time finishing garbage chances. I remember in 1992 when we played against William and Mary in an NCAA playoff game. John Daly's team played well. And what John said in the press conference was the absolute truth. He said, "You know, I don't think they really scored a truly great goal." And we didn't. All we did was frame the goal well. All the balls that were going wide, we redirected in. Any ball the goalkeeper parried, we redirected in. It was our Garbage Box Organization that allowed us to finish many chances. Box organization is something we focus on constantly. Our philosophy is that we're just playing percentages. And a goal that Kristine Lilly scores by sliding in at the far post to redirect a shot going wide counts as much as Mia Hamm weaving through a maze of defenders and ripping one into the upper corner. The big difference is that you might be able to coach that first kind of goal after two or three weeks. But that second kind of goal can only be recruited into your program. We try to score both ways.

From the game perspective, if you don't have good box organization and you end up scoring a goal, it's a fluke, a miss-clearance, a coincidence, or the ball is just hit to where you're going to be. You can win some games on flukes, but at North Carolina we are interested in figuring out ways to win forever. That is with or without great strikers, and that's the challenge. A Mia Hamm and a Kristine Lilly and an April Heinrichs just don't come along all that often. Those are players you can give the ball to and they beat defenses on their own consistently. They don't need any help. But those kinds of strikers are incredibly rare. You have to figure out a system for your front line and midfield to create goals without this rare one v one ability of a Hamm, Lilly, or Heinrichs. Our challenge was actually the fall of 1991. Our forward line was shredded because Mia Hamm and Kristine Lilly were playing for the United States in the first Women's World Championship in China. Our forward line was the previous year's left back, Stacey Blazo, at right wing; Jane Vest, our center half, was at center forward; and Page Coley, our reserve midfielder, was at left wing. Our attack was centered around getting corner kicks and serving it up in the air to the incomparable Tisha Venturini to redirect on goal. This was the beginning of "Framing the Goal" which evolved into such a goal-scoring base for us, Jerry Smith, as I mentioned earlier, was commenting on it three years later.

In box organization, framing the goal or finding seams, there has to be an organizational precision. Obviously, an experienced player — because they have been in these situations so often — is reading what to do and where to run. The timing of it is based on having made hundreds of mistakes so they can now get it right. What we try to do with our box organization is share with the players the benefit of our experience and point out where the majority of the loose balls have ended up. Then we try to get players in those positions, and get them to time their runs to be in certain spaces. Fundamental box organization is to have a choreography based on your knowledge and experience as a coach. You imprint on them the benefit of your experience. That is a very important aspect of coaching — convincing an inexperienced player what to do based on what you have seen. When you get to a higher level and start talking about finding seams, you are talking about a different level of the game. Finding seams is not choreographed. A near-far-slot endline box organization is choreographic. Framing the goal is choreographic, and by that I mean there is a set pattern and a set position where you want players based on where the ball typically ends up. Going into the 1991 World Championship, we had an understanding of fundamental box organization and box choreography. I think our understanding actually was very good. It gave us an attacking structure that our very talented team used as a base for their own creativity and flair. Finding seams is a higher level of box organization. It is the level with which current men's national teams play. Based on the positioning of defenders and the positioning of the ball, you want to time your runs so you get to a space when the ball gets there. You want to end up in the seams within the opposition's defense. These seams are between defenders, or between a defender and a goalkeeper, and there may be two seams between three defenders. These seams are always changing, and because they are changing they can't be choreographed. They have to be recognized. There are a lot of variables involved in finding seams. The 1991 World Championship team was starting to evolve to that next attacking level, but it was actually post-World Cup that we started working on it in earnest.

There has to be a certain precision in box organization. In choreographic box organization, the coach can tell the player where she starts from and where she should end up. In the near-far-slot organization, for the slot player — which is usually the central midfielder running out of midfield to the penalty spot — you have to tell them where you want them to end up and when you want them to get there. The same with the near-post runner. With the far-post runner, however, you have to tell them from where you want them to start, so when the ball is served they are in the correct position to start their run. Framing the goal choreography also is pretty straight-forward. When the shot is being taken, one player runs at near post, one runs at the far-post and one at the goalkeeper. That's pretty simple, but only because experience has told us that a great many balls go just wide. In fact, goalkeepers are trained to parry the ball wide. Though a challenge to organize, this is still very basic because the runs don't require an idea, just timing. You have evolved once you and your players understand the concept of seams and how to find them with or without the ball. To understand the concept of seams, you need an idea, which some players will struggle to get. That was my challenge post-1991 World Cup with the U.S. team and my college team now.

CAROLINA
GOAL !!

IRWIN BELK TRACK
FETZER FIELD

Photo by Andrew Cline

V

Appendix

Chapter 16
Manager's Stat Pack

This packet has an interesting history. I have been manager of the University of North Carolina Women's Soccer Team since 1991. Before becoming manager, I kept stats on the team as a fan in the stands. After joining the team, I was only too eager to adopt the role of statistician. .

Initially, the team had five or six drills for which we took data. I used a legal pad and a calculator and spent many hours on the computer to achieve a finished product. Through an evolution of sorts and much trial and error, I developed this packet, which has made the statistical program more efficient. Consequently, new ways of taking and processing data are popping up each day. We now use about fifteen sets of data during the regular season and six to seven sets during the off-season. I believe that in some small way, they contribute to the proud tradition we have here at UNC.

The success of our team has led many coaches to request this information and emulate our training techniques. In fact, one of Anson's motivations for including this packet in the book is because of its popularity. I hope this information will make it easier for you to record the statistics of competitive training environments. The packet includes data sheets, descriptions of the drills for which they are used and explanations of the data obtained. Anson selected a collection of practice rankings from September of 1994 to show you what would be posted on the board and also the scratch sheets used to collect data before I added the wins and losses to the cumulative daily player rankings. In some cases, to protect the identity of some of the women, we have substituted "Player" for the actual name of the player.

I hope this information is beneficial to all who use it.

Sincerely,
Tom Sander, Manager, University of North Carolina Women's Soccer

Contents

Individual Drill Description: including a description sheet, an example of how the stat sheet is used, and an example of how the stats are posted.

104

The Cooper is an aerobic fitness test with a dual purpose. The players know they will have to do the test when they arrive in preseason, so one purpose of the Cooper is to make sure the players do aerobic fitness coming into the season. It also tests the lungs of a player in the preseason and gives her and the coaching staff an assessment of her general aerobic fitness. The standard all the players are expected to make is to run 7 1/4 laps in 12 minutes. Players 23 and 24, who "Did Not Start," were Tisha Venturini and Angela Kelly, who came to camp late. They both passed in their first attempt. If we count the four keepers who passed, 13 out of 28 players passed on their first attempt. Historically, this is solid. Of the 15 players who failed, eight were walk-ons, so seven recruited players failed the initial test.

Players are ranked based on the number of laps completed in 12 minutes. Only those above the line (#s 1-7) passed the standard. DNF = did not finish (dropped out). DNS = did not start (was not present, was sick, or injured). Injured = injured in running of test. Keepers are listed separately because they have a different standard, 6 3/4. Ties in rank (Confer, Fettig, and Uritus) are listed alphabetically. With all the names clearly listed, this is what would be posted on the team bulletin board the day after the test.

······● Cooper Fitness Test

1st Cooper Run 8/17/94

	Distance
1. Sanchez	7 7/8
2. Burns	7 1/2
3. Egan	7 3/8
3. Keller	7 3/8
3. Roberts	7 3/8
6 Santana	7 1/4 ++
7. Wilson	7 1/4 +
8. Dacey	7 1/8 +
8. Johnson	7 1/8 +
10. Confer	7
10. Fettig	7
10. Uritus	7
Player 13	6 7/8
Player 13	6 7/8
Player 13	6 7/8
Player 16	6 3/4
Player 16	6 3/4
Player 18	6 5/8
Player 19	6 1/2
Player 20	6 3/8
Player 21	DNF
Player 22	Injured
Player 23	DNS
Player 24	DNS
Keepers	
1. Eames	7 1/2
2. Noonan	7 1/4 ++
3. Finger	6 7/8
3. Trojak	6 7/8

Cooper Fitness Test ● ● ● ● ● ●

When the 12 minutes is up, the players stop where they are and their lap positions are recorded as shown on this sheet. Pluses and minuses are used to indicate gradations between whole fractions. We place cones around the track at 1/8 intervals to help us sort out where they finish. I start them off and call out "10 Seconds Under, Five Seconds Under, Pace, Five Seconds Over, 10 Seconds Over" as they run past me. I walk to the 1/4-lap distance. I have discovered the greatest motivator is with two minutes left — rather than giving them an over/under — start a countdown: "Two minutes! ... 1:55 ... 1:50", etc., down to 10, 9, 8, 7, 6, 5, 4, 3, 2, 1. Then I blow the whistle for everyone to stop and we record their distance and rank their order of finish.

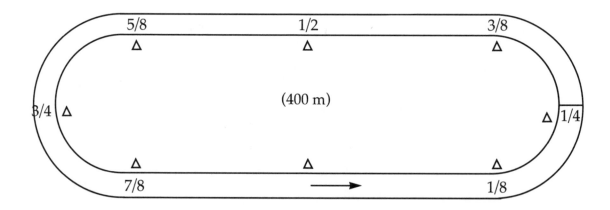

Cooper Fitness Test

Set up: 1. An oval track with one lap equaling 400 meters.

Play: 1. The field players are required to do 7 1/4 laps in 12 minutes.
2. The keepers are required to do 6 3/4 laps in 12 minutes.
3. The following are lap times for both groups:

Field players:	lap	time		Keepers:	lap	time
	1	1:39			1	1:46
	2	3:18			2	3:32
	3	4:57			3	5:18
	4	6:36			4	7:04
	5	8:15			5	8:50
	6	9:54			6	10:36
	7	11:33			6 3/4	12:00
	7 1/4	12:00				

This test is given the day after the Cooper to ensure players did their interval training in the summer. We used to have problems with pulled muscles in pre-season before we added this as a test. We learned the players feared the Cooper Test so much their summer training would only involve distance running as a preparation for the season. So when they started to sprint and change direc-

tions, their bodies could not take it. The 120s are used primarily to improve aerobic fitness. The aerobic fitness is built during the recovery jog back from the sprint. The aerobic part can be seen in the work-to-rest interval ratio of about 1-to-3. The 120s do have a small anaerobic component. The anaerobic component (sprint) is a local muscle endurance builder.

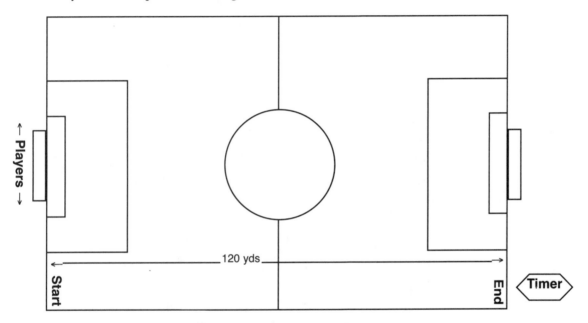

Set up: 1. Players line up at one end of the 120 yard stretch.
2. The timer and recorder stand at the other end of the field.

Play: 1. The timer starts the run by dropping his arm.
2. The timer calls out "5" at five seconds, "10" at ten seconds, and then each second from 15 until the last person crosses the finish line.
3. Players get anywhere from 17 to 20 seconds per run depending on the goals of the coach/team.
4. Players get 60 seconds to jog back to the starting line before the next sprint begins.
5. Ten runs are made with an extra 15 seconds of rest after the 4th and 7th runs (the most popular times for a rest).
6. Keepers are not required to participate.
7. Make-up runs are run immediately after the first 10 are finished, usually on a 1 to 1 ratio (if a player does not cross the finish line within 18 seconds, a make-up run must be run).

120s Results

Rank/Player

1. Brooks
1. Burns
1. Egan
1. Keller
1. Kelly
1. Roberts
1. Sanchez
1. Uritus
1. Venturini
1. Wilson
11. Player 20
11. Player 22
13. Player 21
14. Player 19
15. Player 18
16. Player 17
17. Player 16
18. Player 14
19. Player 13
20. Player 15
21. Player 12
21. Player 11

DNS (Injured)
Boyle

Did Not Run
Keepers

Everyone that passes all 10 sprints in the required time gets a "1" ranking. All others are then ranked based on the number of runs missed and skipped. In the case of two players missing three runs, the player that missed them later in the session (No. 7, 8, and 9 vs. No. 4, 5 and 8) is ranked higher because she went further on her fitness base. If both missed the same runs they are listed alphabetically. Skips can also be determining factors. Ultimately it is up to the person who is compiling the data. DNS and DNR are listed at the bottom. The composite is a list of all sessions so the coach can observe the progress (or regression) of a player's fitness.

120s on 9/6/94   Runs Completed: (1) (2) (3) (4) (5) (6) (7) (8) (9) (10)

Name	Run Missed	# Runs Missed		Makeups
Player 11	(1)(2̶)(3̶)(4)(5)(6)(7̶)(8̶)(9̶)(1̶0̶)	7	[5]	(x)(x)(x)(x)(x)( )( )
Player 12	(1)(2̶)(3)(4)(5̶)(6̶)(7̶)(8)(9̶)(1̶0̶)	7	[5]	(x)(x)(x)(x)(x)( )( )
Player 13	(1)(2)(3)(4)(5̶)(6̶)(7̶)(8)(<u>9</u>)(10)	4 +1 skip	[3]	(x)(x)( )(x)( )( )( )
Player 14	(1)(2)(3)(4)(5̶)(6̶)(7̶)(8)(9̶)(10)	5	[4]	(x)(x)(x)(x)( )( )( )
Player 15	(1)(2)(3)(4)(5̶)(6̶)(7̶)(8)(9̶)(1̶0̶)	6	[4]	(x)(x)(x)(x)( )( )( )
Player 16	(1)(2)(3)(4)(5)(6̶)(7̶)(8)(<u>9</u>)(10)	3 +1 skip	[3]	(x)(x)(x)( )( )( )( )
Player 17	(1)(2)(3)(4)(5)(6̶)(7̶)(8)(9̶)(10)	4	[3]	(x)(x)(x)( )( )( )( )
Player 18	(1)(2)(3)(4)(5)(6)(7̶)(8)(<u>9</u>)(10)	2 +1 skip	[3]	(x)(x)(x)( )( )( )( )
Player 20	(1)(2)(3)(4)(5)(6)(7)(8)(9̶)(10)	1	[1]	(x)( )( )( )( )( )( )
Player 21	(1)(2)(3)(4)(5)(6)(7)(8)(9̶)(1̶0̶)	2	[2]	(x)(x)( )( )( )( )( )
Player 22	(1)(2)(3)(4)(5)(6)(7)(8)(9̶)(10)	1	[1]	(x)( ) ( )( )( )( )( )
Player 19	(1)(2)(3)(4)(5)(6)(7̶)(8)(9̶)(10)	3	[2]	(x)(x)( )( )( )( )( )

underlined = skip

DNS
<u>Boyle</u>
_____
_____
_____
_____
_____
_____

DNR
<u>Keepers</u>
_____
_____
_____
_____
_____
_____

As a run is completed, it is marked off in the upper right. As a player misses a run, her name is recorded and the run she missed is noted. A skip is noted differently (in this case it's underlined). After all 10 runs, the total number of runs missed is written under # runs missed. The coach then determines how many make-up runs are required for each player. Usually it is one for one up to three misses, then four or five make-ups becomes the maximum for any amount of misses (fatigue sets in). The number of make-ups is arbitrary and up to the discretion of the coach. Skipped runs require two make-up runs each. Make-up runs are noted in brackets [ ] and marked off as they are completed by each player. The player is then checked off when she is finished. DNS = did not start (because of injury, sickness, etc.). DNR = did not run (not required to run, as keepers are).

120s •••••

120's Fitness Composite

8/18/1994 (10)*	8/27/1994 (10)	9/6/1994 (10)	9/13/1994 (8)	10/4/1994 (10)
1. Boyle (10)	1. Burns (10)	1. Brooks (10)	1. Venturini (9)**	1. Sanchez (12)
1. Burns (10)	1. Confer (10)	1. Burns (10)	1. Boyle (8)	1. Venturini (12)
1. Confer (10)	1. Egan (10)	1. Egan (10)	1. Brooks (8)	3. Burns 9 (12)
1. Crow (10)	1. Fettig (10)	1. Keller (10)	1. Burns (8)	3. Confer 9 (12)
1. Egan (10)	1. Keller (10)	1. Kelly (10)	1. Byers (8)	3. Egan 9 (12)
1. Keller (10)	1. Kelly (10)	1. Roberts (10)	1. Confer (8)	3. Fettig 9 (12)
1. Roberts (10)	1. Roberts (10)	1. Sanchez (10)	1. Dacey (8)	3. Green 9 (12)
1. Sanchez (10)	1. Sanchez (10)	1. Uritus (10)	1. Egan (8)	3. Johnson 9 (12)
1. Santana (10)	1. Santana (10)	1. Venturini (10)	1. Falk (8)	3. Keller 9 (12)
1. Uritus (10)	1. Venturini (10)	1. Wilson (10)	1. Fettig (8)	3. Kelly 9 (12)
1. Wilson (10)	1. Wilson (10)	11. Player 11	1. Green (8)	3. Roberts 9 (12)
12. Player 12	12. Player 12	11. Player 12	1. Hutton (8)	3. Santana 9 (12)
13. Player 13	12. Player 13	13. Player 13	1. Johnson (8)	3. Wilson 9 (12)
14. Player 14	14. Player 14	14. Player 14	1. Keller 7 (8)	14. Player 14
14. Player 15	14. Player 15	15. Player 15)	1. Kelly (8)	14. Player 15
16. Player 16	16. Player 16	16. Player 16	1. Roberts (8)	14. Player 16
16. Player 17	17. Player 17	17. Player 17	1. Rubio (8)	17. Player 17
18. Player 18	18. Player 18	18. Player 18	1. Sanchez (8)	18. Player 18
18. Player 19	19. Player 19	19. Player 19	1. Santana (8)	19. Player 19
	20. Player 20	20. Player 20	1. Uritus (8)	19. Player 20
DNS Byers	21. Player 21	21. Player 21	1. Wilson (8)	21. Player 21
DNS Falk	21. Player 22)	21. Player 22	22. Player 22	
	DNS Brooks	DNS Boyle	DNS Crow	DNS Crow, Uritus

* (# runs required that day)

Format: Name, runs made out of required (total runs made, including makeups)

** — On this day, we only required eight runs, but we assigned each player a teammate. Basically, we tied (figuratively, not literally) our fittest player with our least fit on down the line. Here Venturini, one of our fittest, was tied to a player who failed to make all eight runs, so Venturini ran an extra one for her. This was an experiment with social pressure to get everyone to pass. As you can see, with one exception it worked.

Cones is used about two-thirds of the way through the season, replacing 120s because it involves more soccer elements. This drill serves to hone the anaerobic fitness and agility base of a player. The agility is improved through the changes in direction that have to be made at speed. The anaerobic fitness of a player is increased as local muscle endurance is made even stronger. This is achieved through a work-to-rest interval ratio more soccer-specific than 120s can provide. The ratio is a little tougher than 1-to-1 with runs lasting 35 to 40 seconds and recovery being only the remainder of that minute (25 or 20 seconds).

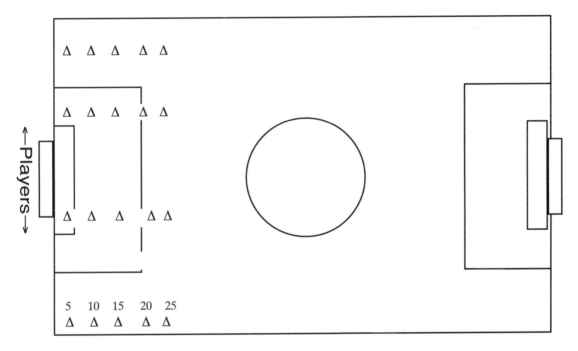

Set up: 1. Players line up along an endline.

          2. Five cones are placed at five-yard intervals from the endline out to 25 yards.

Play: 1. When the timer starts the drill, the players have to run out to the first cone and back, out to the second cone and back, out to the third cone and back and so on.

          2. They have either 35 or 40 seconds to complete this run, depending on the abilities of the players and goals of the team as determined by the coach. A combination of 35's and 40's can be used, increasing the number of 35's as the team gets more fit.

          3. Players have 25 seconds to recuperate after 35-second runs and 20 seconds to recuperate after 40-second runs.

          4. We start out with 6 in 35 and 4 in 40 and try to work our way up to 10 in 35 by the NCAA Final Four.

          5. Extra 15 seconds of rest between 4 and 7.

Cones • • • • ••

Cones
11/22/94

Rank/Player

1. Burns
1. Dacey
1. Egan
1. Falk
1. Green
1. Johnson
1. Keller
1. Kelly
1. Roberts
1. Sanchez
1. Venturini
1. Wilson
1. Rubio
1. Uritus
1. Santana
16. Player 18
16. Player 16
18. Player 17

DNS
Player 19 (120s)
Player 20 (120s)
Player 21 (120s)
Player 22 (120s)
Player 23 (absent)

DNR
Keepers

Parameters:
9 in :35;
No. 5 in :40
rest @ 3 and 7

Everyone that passes all 10 sprints in the required time gets a "1" ranking. All others are then ranked based on the number of runs missed and skipped. In the case of two players missing three runs, the player that missed them later in the session (No. 7, 8 and 9 vs. 4, 5 and 8) is ranked higher because she went further in her fitness base. If both missed the same runs then they are listed alphabetically. Skips can also be determining factors. Ultimately, it is up to the person who is compiling the data. DNS and DNR are listed at the bottom. The composite is a list of all sessions so the coach can observe the progress (or regression) of a player's fitness.

Cones on 11/22/94   Runs Completed: (1) (2) (3)· (4) (5) (6) (7)· (8) (9) (10)

Name	Run Missed	# Runs Missed	Makeups
Player 16	(1) (2) (3) (4) (5) (6̶) (7) (8) (9) (10)	1	(x) ( ) ( ) ( ) ( ) ( ) ( )√
Player 17	(1) (2) (3) (4) (5) (6̶) (7̶) (8) (9) (10)	2	(x) (x) ( ) ( ) ( ) ( ) ( )√
Player 18	(1) (2) (3) (4) (5) (6) (7̶) (8) (9) (10)	1	(x) ( ) ( ) ( ) ( ) ( ) ( )√
	(1) (2) (3) (4) (5) (6) (7) (8) (9) (10)		( ) ( ) ( ) ( ) ( ) ( ) ( )
	(1) (2) (3) (4) (5) (6) (7) (8) (9) (10)		( ) ( ) ( ) ( ) ( ) ( ) ( )
	(1) (2) (3) (4) (5) (6) (7) (8) (9) (10)		( ) ( ) ( ) ( ) ( ) ( ) ( )
	(1) (2) (3) (4) (5) (6) (7) (8) (9) (10)		( ) ( ) ( ) ( ) ( ) ( ) ( )
	(1) (2) (3) (4) (5) (6) (7) (8) (9) (10)		( ) ( ) ( ) ( ) ( ) ( ) ( )
	(1) (2) (3) (4) (5) (6) (7) (8) (9) (10)		( ) ( ) ( ) ( ) ( ) ( ) ( )
	(1) (2) (3) (4) (5) (6) (7) (8) (9) (10)		( ) ( ) ( ) ( ) ( ) ( ) ( )
	(1) (2) (3) (4) (5) (6) (7) (8) (9) (10)		( ) ( ) ( ) ( ) ( ) ( ) ( )
	(1) (2) (3) (4) (5) (6) (7) (8) (9) (10)		( ) ( ) ( ) ( ) ( ) ( ) ( )
	(1) (2) (3) (4) (5) (6) (7) (8) (9) (10)		( ) ( ) ( ) ( ) ( ) ( ) ( )
	(1) (2) (3) (4) (5) (6) (7) (8) (9) (10)		( ) ( ) ( ) ( ) ( ) ( ) ( )

DNS   DNR

Byers_____

Brooks_____

Confer_____

Hutton_____

Riggs_____

_____

_____

Keepers: DID NOT RUN

_____

_____

_____

_____

_____

_____

Like in 120s, as a run is completed, it's marked off in the upper right. Thirty-fives and 40's indicate times for each run. Bullets (•) indicate extra rests. As a player misses a run, her name is recorded and the run she missed is noted with a slash through the number. A skip is noted differently (it could be an X). After all 10 runs, the total number of runs missed is written under # runs missed. The coach then determines how many makeup runs are required for each player. Usually it is one for one up to three misses, then four or five make-ups becomes the maximum for any amount of misses (fatigue sets in). The number of make-ups is up to the discretion of the coach. Skipped runs require two make-up runs each. Make-up runs are noted and marked off as they are completed by each player. The player is then checked off when she is finished. DNS = did not start (because of injury, sickness, etc). DNR = did not run (not required to run. In this session, our goalkeepers did not run).

Three Tier Shooting • • • • •

Three Tier Shooting is a pure finishing exercise. The great thing about the drill is it gives a player the chance to practice three types of finishing with the three balls that are served. Three Tier Shooting is used immediately after every fitness session (120s, Cones) as a recovery exercise. This forces a player to focus on finishing a shot while fatigued, a necessity in exhausting games and overtime periods. Focus, while you are physically shredded, can prove to be the deciding element in achieving victory.

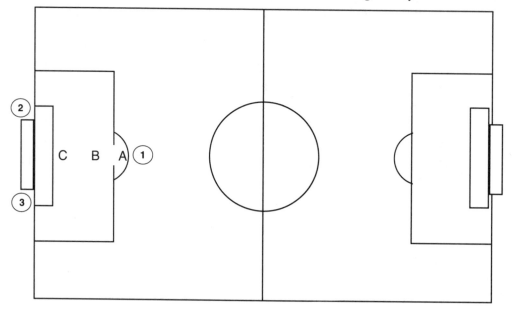

Set up: 1. First third of alphabetical roster lines up at 1 outside of the "D".

2. Second third of alphabetical roster lines up at 2.

3. Last third of alphabetical roster lines up at 3.

4. All balls are divided equally between the 1, 2 and 3 groups.

Play: 1. Player at 1 launches a shot from the top of the "D" before A.

2. Player at 2 passes a ball out when player from 1 strikes the first ball so that the player from 1 (running toward goal) can shoot on the run from B.

3. Player at 3 immediately tosses a ball at head level so player from 1 (still running) can head the ball from C at the 6 yard line.

4. Player from 1 then retrieves a ball and gets in line at 2

5. Players from 2 rotate to 3 after passing the ball out to player running from 1.

6. Players from 3 rotate to 1 after tossing ball to player running from 1.

7. Keepers usually switch halfway through the roster since the pace is constant as players continually rotate and make their runs.

8. All players go through the drill (three shots) three to four times.

9. Each shot is recorded as a (+) or (-) on the stat sheet as it is taken (see sheets).

114

3 Tier Shooting on 9/13/94

Roster	Long				Finesse				Head				L	F	H	G.Attempt
	1	2	3	4	1	2	3	4	1	2	3	4				
Boyle	-	-	-		-	-	-		-	+	+		0	0	2	2/9
Brooks	+	-	-		-	-	-		-	+	-		1	0	1	2/9
Burns	-	-	-		-	+	-		+	-	+		0	1	2	3/9
Byers	-	-	-		+	+	-		+	-	-		0	2	1	3/9
Confer	-	-	-		-	-	+		+	-	+		0	1	2	3/9
Crow	-INJURED															
Dacey	-	+	+		+	-	+		+	-	+		2	2	2	6/9
Egan	-	-	-		+	-	+		-	-	+		0	2	1	3/9
Falk	-	-	+		+	+	-		+	+	+		1	2	3	6/9
Fettig	-	+	-		+	+	+		-	+	+		1	3	2	6/9
Green	-	-	-		-	-	-		+	-	+		0	0	2	2/9
Hutton	-	-	-		-	+	+		-	+	-		0	2	1	3/9
Johnson	-	-	-		+	-	-		-	-	+		0	1	1	2/9
Keller	-	-	-		+	+	+		-	+	+		0	3	2	5/9
Kelly	-	-	-		+	-	-		-	-	-		0	1	0	1/9
Riggs	-	+	-		+	-	+		+	-	-		1	2	1	4/9
Roberts	-	-	-		-	-	-		+	+	-		0	0	2	2/9
Rubio	-	-	-		+	+	-		+	-	-		0	2	1	3/9
Sanchez	-	-	-		-	+	-		+	-	+		0	1	2	3/9
Santana	-	-	-		+	-	-		+	-	+		0	1	2	3/9
Uritus	-	+	-		+	+	+		+	-	+		1	3	2	6/9
Venturini	-	+	+		-	+	+		-	+	+		2	2	2	6/9
Wilson	-	-	-		-	-	+		-	-	-		0	1	0	1/9

Keepers	Allowed/Attempts		Keeper Changes
Eames	11/33	.333	1st series: Finger: Boyle thru Hutton; Noonan: Johnson-Wilson
Finger	24/66	.363	2nd series: Trojak: Boyle-Hutton; Eames: Johnson-Wilson
Noonan	28/66	.424	3rd series: Noonan: Boyle-Hutton; Finger: Johnson-Wilson
Trojak	12/33	.363	

A (+) indicates a goal and a (-) indicates a missed shot. 1,2,3 and 4 indicate the series. There is a Long, Finesse and a Head shot for each series. So as a player makes her run, she will get a mark under the 1 in Long, under the 1 in Finesse, and under the 1 in Head. Each player is recorded the same way until the roster is run. Then the next shots are recorded under 2 in each shot column since it is the second series. For example: Boyle missed all three shots on her first series (minuses in all 1 columns). But on the second and third series she made the header (+ in 2nd and 3rd series under Head).

Three Tier Shooting • • • • •

Three Tier Shooting
9/13/94

Rank/Player	Made	Taken	%Made	Long	Finesse	Head
1. Venturini	15	27	55.6	2	6	7
1. Falk	15	27	55.6	2	4	9
3. Confer	19	39	48.7	4	6	9
3. Uritus	19	39	48.7	2	9	8
5. Dacey	18	39	46.2	2	8	8
5. Keller	18	39	46.2	1	6	11
7. Wilson	16	36	44.4	2	5	9
9. Riggs	17	39	43.6	3	7	7
9. Fettig	17	39	43.6	3	6	8
9. Hutton	17	39	43.6	1	6	10
12. Egan	15	39	38.5	2	7	6
12. Sanchez	15	39	38.5	1	6	8
14. Boyle	11	30	36.7	1	5	5
15. Player 15	13	39	33.3	1	4	8
16. Player 16	12	39	30.8	1	3	8
17. Player 17	8	27	29.6	1	2	5
18. Player 18	8	30	26.7	1	2	5
19. Player 19	10	39	25.6	0	4	6
19. Player 20	10	39	25.6	0	4	6
21. Player 21	9	39	23.1	0	4	5
22. Player 22	8	39	20.5	2	3	3
22. Player 23	8	39	20.5	2	2	4

Rank/Keeper	Allow	Attempts	%Allowed
1. Trojak	57	159	35.8
2. Finger	95	252	37.7
3. Keeper 3	62	162	38.3
4. Keeper 4	102	258	39.5

The rankings are based on a pure percentage mark. It is the number of shots made divided by the number taken. In the case of a tie, the player with more long shots, or finesse shots is ranked higher since this implies greater ability. Long, Finesse, and Head are posted to show the strengths and weaknesses of each player's shot. Keepers are ranked by their percent allowed, lowest to highest. Again, it is a pure percentage. The whole statistic is cumulative and updated each time the drill is done.

One v Ones on 9/7/94

One v One (or Top Gun) is the primary competitive matrix because all soccer boils down to the one v one duel. The player must be able to beat her opponent and stop her opponent in the one v one confrontation. This drill involves all four components necessary to win games. The player must have some tactical understanding of how to match up her best qualities against her opponent's weaknesses. For example, a faster opponent should try to draw a slower opponent away from the cone. Fitness is a critical factor in one v ones since the players are in a furious battle for three-minute stretches. Psychological toughness is an extremely important component of the drill because it's just you and your opponent — Who is going to crack? The two things that factor into winning a game more than anything are a player's physical and psychological domination of her opponent. And, obviously, your one v one attacking flair, your technical ability with the ball and your skill at going through someone all contribute to your success. This drill serves to harden many aspects of a player's game.

Roster	W	L	T
Boyle	0	0	3
Brooks	0	0	3
Burns	0	1	2
Byers	1	0	2
Confer	0	0	3
Crow	0	2	1
Dacey	1	0	2
Egan	2	1	0
Falk	2	0	1
Fettig	1	0	2
Green	0	0	3
Hutton	0	1	2
Johnson	0	2	1
Keller	2	1	0
Kelly	2	0	1
Riggs	0	1	2
Roberts	1	1	1
Rubio	0	2	1
Sanchez	0	2	1
Santana	2	0	1
Uritus	0	1	2
Venturini	1	0	2
Wilson	0	0	0

Keepers			
Eames	1	1	1
Finger	1	0	2
Noonan	1	2	0
Trojak	1	1	1

This is pretty straight-forward, just a format we use to record the 1 v1 rankings during one practice.

One v Ones •••••

Top Gun
9/7/94

Rank/Player	% Won	Win	Loss	Tie
1. Egan	87.5	10	1	1
2. Keller	87.5	10	1	1
3. Santana	79.2	7	0	5
4. Kelly	77.8	5	0	4
5. Fettig	66.7	6	2	4
5. Wilson	66.7	4	1	4
7. Riggs	55.6	3	2	4
7. Venturini	55.6	3	2	4
9. Confer	54.2	5	4	3
9. Roberts	54.2	5	4	3
9. Sanchez	54.2	5	4	3
12. Player 12	50.0	4	4	4
12. Player 13	50.0	4	4	4
12. Player 14	50.0	3	3	6
15. Player 15	45.8	2	3	7
16. Player 16	44.4	2	3	4
17. Player 17	41.7	2	3	1
18. Player 18	37.5	1	4	7
19. Player 19	33.3	1	5	6
20. Player 20	27.8	1	5	3
21. Player 21	25.0	0	6	6
22. Player 22	16.7	0	8	4
23. Player 23	8.3	0	10	2

Keepers				
1. Finger	75.0	7	1	4
2. Noonan	58.3	6	4	2
3. Keeper 3	44.4	3	4	2
4. Keeper 4	25.0	2	8	2

This statistic is also cumulative. The percentage won is calculated by counting ties as one-half of a win. For example: Egan with 10 wins and one tie gets 10.5 wins out of 12 battles, or a 87.5 winning percentage. The players are ranked highest to lowest based on percent won. Again, this is cumulative for the season. Ties (in ranking) are settled by giving preference to the player with the most wins/least losses/more times competed.

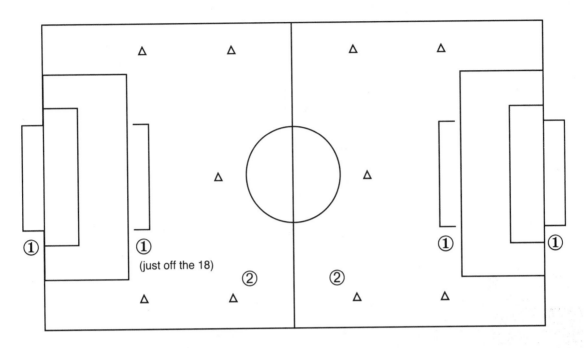

Set up: 1. One pair of opposing goals (1) is placed at each end of the field according to the diagram (about 22 yards apart).

2. Ten cones (2) are spaced at intervals around the playing field.

3. Pairs of players are assigned to each cone according to a matrix (following) that rotates players so that they play everyone at least once in the season.

   A. Strikers and attacking midfielders play in goals at ends of field as often as possible (distribution of player pairs on field is up to individual coach).

   B. Keepers play in goals and switch goals half-way through each 1 v 1 battle.

Play: 1. Play lasts two to three minutes (at discretion of coach).

2. Players try to hit the cone with the ball by "beating" the other player 1 v 1.

3. Players attack and defend the same cone, the larger the cone the better.

4. One point is earned by a player for each hit and then ball changes possession.

5. Missed shots must be chased by both players – no cone hanging!

6. Each session consists of three battles of two to three minutes each.

7. Players in goals shoot for goals instead of cones.

8. Keepers switch goals half-way through the drill.

9. At the end of the session (after three battles) the players report their record in win-loss-tie format. Players are encouraged to keep score out loud to avoid controversy, and they are asked to agree on the score after each game.

Soccer 1 v 1 matrix

Day 1	Day 2	Day 3	Day 4	Day 5	Day 6	Day 7	Day 8	Day 9
1 v 2	1 v 4	1 v 6	1 v 8	1 v 10	1 v 12	1 v 14	1 v 16	1 v 18
3 v 4	2 v 6	4 v 8	6 v 10	8 v 12	10 v 14	12 v 16	14 v 18	16 v 20
5 v 6	3 v 8	2 v 10	4 v 12	6 v 14	8 v 16	10 v 18	12 v 20	14 v 22
7 v 8	5 v 10	3 v 12	2 v 14	4 v 16	6 v 18	8 v 20	10 v 22	12 v 24
9 v 10	7 v 12	5 v 14	3 v 16	2 v 18	4 v 20	6 v 22	8 v 24	10 v 23
11 v 12	9 v 14	7 v 16	5 v 18	3 v 20	2 v 22	4 v 24	6 v 23	8 v 21
13 v 14	11 v 16	9 v 18	7 v 20	5 v 22	3 v 24	2 v 23	4 v 21	6 v 19
15 v 16	13 v 18	11 v 20	9 v 22	7 v 24	5 v 23	3 v 21	2 v 19	4 v 17
17 v 18	15 v 20	13 v 22	11 v 24	9 v 23	7 v 21	5 v 19	3 v 17	2 v 15
19 v 20	17 v 22	15 v 24	13 v 23	11 v 21	9 v 19	7 v 17	5 v 15	3 v 13
21 v 22	19 v 24	17 v 23	15 v 21	13 v 19	11 v 17	9 v 15	7 v 13	5 v 11
23 v 24	21 v 23	19 v 21	17 v 19	15 v 17	13 v 15	11 v 13	9 v 11	7 v 9

Day 10	Day 11	Day 12	Day 13	Day 14	Day 15	Day 16	Day 17	Day 18
1 v 20	1 v 22	1 v 24	1 v 23	1 v 21	1 v 19	1 v 17	1 v 15	1 v 13
18 v 22	20 v 24	22 v 23	24 v 21	23 v 19	21 v 17	19 v 15	17 v 13	15 v 11
16 v 24	18 v 23	20 v 21	22 v 19	24 v 17	23 v 25	21 v 13	19 v 11	17 v 9
14 v 23	16 v 21	18 v 19	20 v 17	22 v 15	24 v 15	23 v 11	21 v 9	19 v 7
12 v 21	14 v 19	16 v 17	18 v 15	20 v 13	22 v 11	24 v 9	23 v 7	21 v 5
10 v 19	12 v 17	14 v 15	16 v 13	18 v 11	20 v 9	22 v 7	24 v 5	23 v 3
8 v 17	10 v 15	12 v 13	14 v 11	16 v 9	18 v 7	20 v 5	22 v 3	24 v 2
6 v 5	8 v 13	10 v 11	12 v 9	14 v 7	16 v 5	18 v 3	20 v 2	22 v 4
4 v 13	6 v 11	8 v 9	10 v 7	12 v 5	14 v 3	16 v 2	18 v 4	20 v 6
2 v 11	4 v 9	6 v 7	8 v 5	10 v 3	12 v 2	14 v 4	16 v 6	18 v 8
3 v 9	2 v 7	4 v 5	6 v 3	8 v 2	10 v 4	12 v 6	14 v 8	16 v 10
5 v 7	3 v 5	2 v 3	4 v 2	6 v 4	8 v 6	10 v 8	12 v 10	14 v 12

Day 19	Day 20	Day 21	Day 22	Day 23
1 v 11	1 v 9	1 v 7	1 v 5	1 v 3
13 v 9	11 v 7	9 v 5	7 v 3	5 v 2
15 v 7	13 v 5	11 v 3	9 v 2	7 v 4
17 v 5	15 v 3	13 v 2	11 v 4	9 v 6
19 v 3	17 v 2	15 v 4	13 v 6	11 v 8
21 v 2	19 v 4	17 v 6	15 v 8	13 v 10
23 v 4	21 v 6	19 v 8	17 v 10	15 v 12
24 v 6	23 v 8	21 v 10	19 v 12	17 v 14
22 v 8	24 v 10	23 v 12	21 v 14	19 v 16
20 v 10	22 v 12	24 v 14	23 v 16	21 v 18
18 v 12	20 v 14	22 v 16	24 v 18	23 v 20
16 v 14	18 v 16	20 v 18	22 v 20	24 v 22

Each player is assigned a number in the matrix based on the alphabetical roster of the team. This matrix rotates all numbers around the 1, counter-clockwise (starting with Day 1). A Day indicates the pairings for a two- or three-minute battle. Circled pairs (as determined by coach) are striker/starter pairs to play in goals for a more authentic situation. So before practice, circle the pairs you want competing in the goals with the live keepers, try to pick players that will be responsible for most of your finishing.

"Most competitive" is the name we have given to all the half-field games — 4v4, 3v3, 2v2 — that we play in practice. We even throw in the occasional 11v11. We want the players to believe that they are the reason their team wins — that they are the deciding factor. There are two ways to impact on winning. A player can be a personality and use her own talent and psychological strength to carry the team on her back to victory, or she can lead and organize her team to victory through encouragement and direction. Both of these methods of impacting on the team are critical in the development of high-level winners. The Most Competitive drill and statistics develop and bear out these players.

This category also includes anything else in which they might compete, like this adjacent 2v2 heading competition. We just want everyone to know they should focus, go after it and play to win in every part of practice.

······• Most Competitive

Most Competitive on 9/2/94

(2v2 Heading Pairs)

Wilson/Boyle	(W)
Sanchez/Crow	(L)
Burns/Fettig	(W)
Rubio/Riggs	(L)
Brooks/Green	(W)
Hutton/Uritus	(L)
Roberts/Byers	(L)
Egan/Santana	(W)
Falk/Johnson	(L)
Confer/Brooks	(W)
Venturini/Kelly	(W)
Keller/Dacey	(L)

The players serving each other (teammates) get wins and losses together. For example: Wilson and Boyle both get a win, while Sanchez and Crow (the other two they competed against) both get a loss. This format should not be confused with the heading ladder format where opponents are listed on the same line. In this drill, teammates are listed on the same line.

2 v 2 Heading Pairs

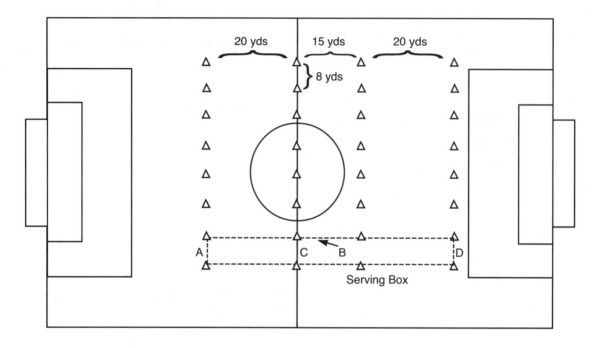

Set up: 1. Cones are set up according to diagram above creating a series of "serving boxes" across the field.

2. Four players are assigned to a box with A and B competing against C and D.

Play: 1. A serves B (teammate).

2. B tries to head the ball back past C who must defend her "goal" (the ball must stay between the cones and below C's head to be a "goal".

3. D then serves C (teammate).

4. C tries to head the ball back past B (same rules apply).

5. Pairs alternate service for a given time period (usually 3 minutes), then B and C serve A and D.

6. Like the Heading Ladder, players get wins, losses, and ties based on goals scored by heading.

**note: cooperation between teammates is necessary to help each other (with good services).

122

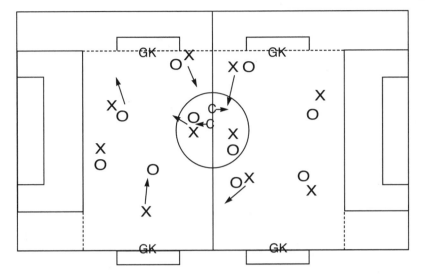

Field shape: 5v5-plus keepers; C=Coach

Set up: 1. (At discretion of coach).

Play: Any scrimmage can be applied to this statistic. It includes 11 v 11, 4 v 4, 5 v 5, etc. The most common "most competitive" training arenas are 5v5 plus keepers. Most popular games? 1) Man-to-man all over the field, and you can only tackle your man; 2) Pass and follow your pass; 3) One touch with a permanent attacker (plus one player); 4) Combination play game (points are given for give and goes, takeovers, double passes); 5) Knock and move game (after every pass, accelerate somewhere). Other popular 5v5 or 6v6 games without keepers is on half a field: 6) Five passes equals one goal, or an even better variation: 7) Five passes equals one goal, short-short-long.

Field shape: 4v4-plus keepers.

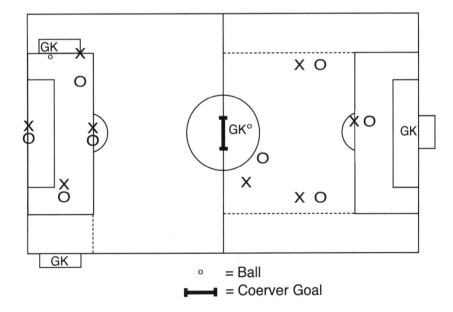

○   = Ball

▬ = Coerver Goal

Most Competitive •••••

Most Competitive on 9/7/94

Team 1   Permanent Attacker   Team 2

_____   _____
_____   _____   _____
_____   _____   _____
_____   _____
_____   _____
_____   _____
_____   _____

(T) (T) ( )   ( ) ( )   (T) (W) ( )
( )   ( ) ( )   ( )

Team 1   Permanent Attacker   Team 2

_____   _____
_____   _____   _____
_____   _____   _____
_____   _____
_____   _____
_____   _____
_____   _____

(L) (L) ( )   ( ) ( )   (W) (T) ( )
( )   ( ) ( )   ( )

Keepers

Eames (L) (W) ( ) ( )   Noonan (L) (W) ( ) ( )

Finger (W) (L) ( ) ( )   Trojak (W) (L) ( ) ( )

Teams get a W, L or T based on the score of the scrimmage. Permanent attackers automatically get a win and are listed separately in the center columns for this purpose. In computing for individuals, each player on the team gets the W, L or T of the team. In the five v fives, plus keepers, the starters play against starters and the reserves play against the reserves, then the winners and losers play off. When a team of starters plays a team of reserves, the reserves begin the game with a one-goal or one-player advantage. Keepers will also switch goals — on the fly —in the middle of the game, and their win-loss is determined by the total goals allowed for that game.

Most Competitive
9/7/94

Rank/Player	% Won	Wins	Losses	Ties
1. Keller	73.8	12	2	7
2. Wilson	73.7	13	4	2
3. Crow	71.4	12	3	6
4. Venturini	66.7	5	2	2
5. Sanchez	59.5	11	7	3
5. Egan	59.5	10	6	5
5. Santana	59.5	10	6	5
8. Burns	54.8	9	7	5
8. Dacey	54.8	8	6	7
8. Confer	54.8	7	5	9
11. Fettig	50.0	9	9	3
12. Player 12	47.6	7	8	6
13. Player 13	45.2	8	10	3
14. Player 14	44.4	2	3	4
15. Player 15	42.9	6	9	6
16. Player 16	40.5	7	11	3
17. Player 17	39.5	6	10	3
18. Player 18	38.1	5	10	6
19. Player 19	37.5	6	11	3
20. Player 20	35.7	2	4	1
21. Player 21	35.3	3	8	6
22. Player 22	31.3	3	9	4
23. Player 23	29.4	4	11	2

Keepers

Rank/Player	% Won	Win	Loss	Tie
1. Trojak	61.4	11	6	5
2. Noonan	60.5	10	6	3
3. Keeper 3	55.3	9	7	3
4. Keeper 4	26.5	3	11	3

Players are ranked based on the percentage of games they win in the small games. Ties count for one-half of a win, therefore Keller's 12 wins and 7 ties (3.5 wins) out of 21 games gives her a 73.8 winning percentage. Like Top Gun (1v1s) ties in the rank are broken by the player with the most wins/least losses/most games played getting preference. Alphabetical order is a last resort.

Heading Ladder • • • ••

The Heading Ladder, like the one v ones to cones, is a technical duel with a powerful psychological element. The players are placed in an intimidating environment where the stronger, more courageous player will win. The drill forces players to overcome their fears and be the intimidator in the duel. It also very realistically replicates the duels in games, and therefore, translates easily to the playing field.

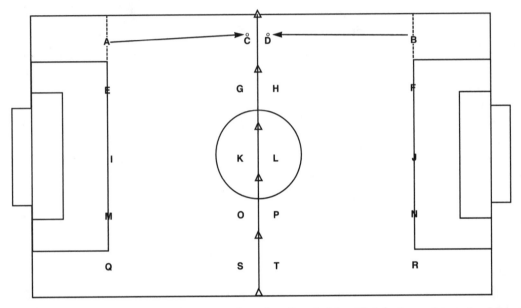

Set up: 1. Players are paired according to rank on heading ladder. Height is used to pair players if it is the first time the drill is used.

2. Player A duels player B and player C duels player D, and so on across the field with A being the tallest player and Z being the shortest.

3. One pair (competing) is on the mid-stripe and the other pair serves balls from the 18-yard lines.

Play: 1. A serves a flighted ball to C and D. C tries to flick the ball past D while D tries to head the ball back toward A.

2. B then serves a flighted ball to C and D. C and D compete again, this time reversing roles as D tries to flick the ball and C tries to head it back to B.

3. After a given time period — usually 3 minutes — the pairs switch so that A competes with B in the "box" and C and D alternate serving balls in.

4. Each player wins or loses based on how many headers she wins. We use the mid-stripe as the dividing line. A win simply means she heads the ball over or past the line and her opponent does not.

5. Wins, losses, and ties are recorded after the drill.

6. Players move up or down the "ladder" based on who they beat or lose to, like a tennis ladder.

(2 v 2 Heading Pairs) For Heading Ladder

Johnson / Confer	(L)	(W)
Uritus / Crow	(W)	(L)
Hutton / Egan	(W)	(L)
Brooks (missed practice)	( )	( )
Venturini / Boyle	(W)	(L)
Kelly / Dacey	(L)	(W)
Player 11 / Player 12	(L)	(W)
Player 13 / Player 14	(W)	(L)
Player 14 / Player 15	(W)	(L)
Player 16 / Player 17	(L)	(W)
Player 18 / Player 19	(W)	(L)
Player 20 / Player 21	(T)	(T)

> The dueling pairs are written down while the players are competing., For example, Johnson vs. Confer, Crow vs. Uritus. Wins and losses are recorded after the competition. To speed up the recording of scores, only the first column is needed (Johnson, Uritus, Hutton, Venturini, etc.). The second column can be extrapolated from the first at a later time (Kelly's loss means Dacey won, and Johnson's win means Confer lost.)

Heading Ladder 9/22/94

Rank	Player	Rank	Player	Rank	Player
1.	Johnson	9.	Boyle	17.	Player 17
2.	Confer	10.	Dacey	18.	Player 18
3.	Uritus	11	Kelly	19.	Player 19
4.	Crow	12.	Player 12	20.	Player 20
5.	Hutton	13.	Player 13	21.	Player 21
6.	Egan	14.	Player 14	22.	Player 22
7.	Brooks	15.	Player 15		
8.	Venturini	16.	Player 16		

> Using the previous heading ladder as the benchmark, wins and losses move players up and down the rankings. Since Dacey beat Kelly, she moves up from No. 11 on last ladder, and Kelly drops from No. 10. Uritus beat Crow, but remained in place because she was No. 3 on the last ladder and Crow was No. 4.

Speed Ladder • • • • • •

The Speed Ladder is used to a small degree to improve the speed of players. More importantly, though, it gives an assessment of their speed and the improvement in their speed throughout the season and their career. It also shows to the coaches a commitment by the player in the off-season to the weight room and in speed training because the ones that work hard move up the ladder from year to year. (Look at Robin Confer's improvement from 1994 to 1995. Her work in the weight room and in speed training in the spring of 1995 were among the most intense on the team). Coaches also find the ladder useful in determining player positions since speed is always a factor up front, on the flank, or in marking positions in the back. It also gives you an accurate picture of who your fastest are if you need to match them up against explosive opponents.

Speed Ladder 9/2/94

Rank Player
1. Boyle
2. Sanchez
3. Brooks
4. Rubio
5. Egan
6. Roberts
7. Wilson
8. Falk
9. Confer
10. Burns
11. Player 11
12. Player 12
13. Player 13
14. Player 14
15. Player 15
16. Player 16
17. Player 17
18. Player 18
19. Player 19
20. Player 20
21. Player 21
22. Player 22
23. Player 23

The players are ranked (without ties) from first to last based on the last finishing order recorded from the running of the speed ladder.

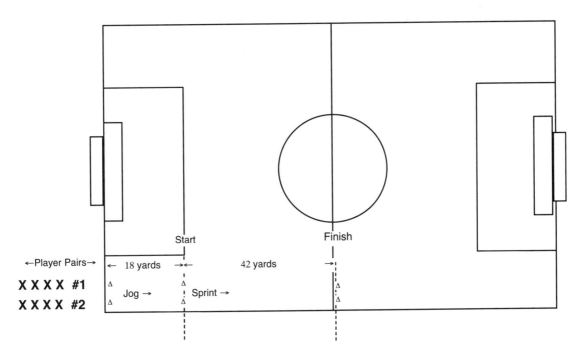

Set Up:
1. Cones spaced about eight feet apart are placed at the endline, at 18-yard line and at the mid-stripe as shown in diagram.
2. Players are paired up according their speed.
   A. Use the current speed ladder to pair No. 1 with No. 2, No. 3 with No. 4, and so on.
   B. If it is the first time using the statistic then pair the players as closely as possible.

Play:
1. Players jog from first cone to second cone.
2. At the second cone, they sprint to the finish at the mid-stripe (the jog gives them a moving start).
3. The person recording the stat is at the finish line writing down the players in order of finish (winner of first pair, then loser, winner of second pair, then loser, and so on through the roster).
4. After the first finishing order is established, the fastest is placed atop the second finishing order and consecutive players are paired up for the second run, but now No. 1 runs alone, No. 2 races No. 3, No. 4 vs. No. 5, and so on down the line
5. This sequence is repeated for additional runs, but now No. 1 races the winner of 2v3; the loser of 2v3 races the winner of 4v5, etc.

Speed Ladder •••••

Speed Ladder on 9/2/94

1st Run Finish Order	**2nd Run Finish Order**	**3rd Run Finish Order**
Boyle	Boyle	
Sanchez	Sanchez	
Brooks	Brooks	
Egan	Rubio	
Rubio	Egan	
Roberts	Roberts	
Wilson	Wilson	
Confer	Falk	
Falk	Confer	
Burns	Burns	
Byers	Byers	
Dacey	Santana	
Player 13	Player 13	
Player 14	Player 14	
Player 15	Player 15	
Player 16	Player 16	
Player 17	Player 17	
Player 18	Player 18	
Player 19	Player 19	
Player 20	Player 20	
Player 21	Player 21	
Player 22	Player 22	

The finishing order is written down as the players cross the finish line. Then the fastest (Boyle) is given the top rank in the second order. The second (Sanchez) and the third (Brooks) are paired to run. The fourth (Egan) and fifth (Rubio) are paired to run, and so on. The second run finish order is recorded as they cross the finish line. Sanchez beat Brooks, Rubio beat Egan, etc., and a new finish order is established. This can continue depending on time/fitness considerations.

Triangle Passing

Triangle Passing measures the technical passing ability of players. It is the best measure of a player's precision in their flighted passing game because it requires the server to hit a moving receiver so accurately that the receiver can take the ball out of the air. The warmup, equally valuable, begins with balls on the ground, using the inside and outside of both feet and bending the ball with the run or into the run.

We also try to teach soccer's passing and trapping rhythm in this exercise. We stress that right after you pass, you accelerate. And while you are preparing your first touch (trapping), you decelerate. We are also constantly telling them to bend their runs when they lay the ball off in order to give the server an easier target and the receiver a more open angle of reception. We are also barking out a litany of <u>Accelerate After the Pass!</u> <u>Decelerate on the First Touch!</u> This acceleration/deceleration rhythm is one of the many rhythms of our game, and I have found this environment one of the best to teach this fundamental but critical nuance.

Roster	Successful Passes
Boyle	8
Brooks	5
Burns	7
Byers	8
Confer	4
Crow	10
Dacey	7
Egan	6
Falk	8
Fettig	9
Green	8
Hutton	9
Johnson	8
Keller	6
Kelly	6
Riggs	6
Roberts	5
Rubio	6
Sanchez	6
Santana	5
Uritus	5
Venturini	6
Wilson	11

Each player is responsible for keeping track of her points out loud. The number of successful passes each player makes is recorded on this single roster type of format.

131

Triangle Passing •••••

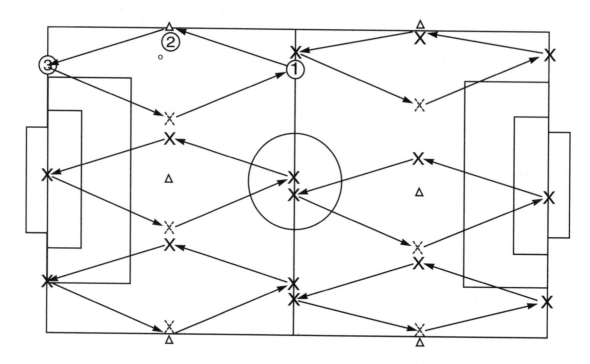

Set up: 1. Players are grouped in threes and arranged in triangles from the endline to the mid-stripe with the third person equidistant from the other two (**1, 2** and **3**)

Play: 1. **2** starts a bending run away from **1**.

2. **1** serves a flighted ball to **2** so it hits **2** at the half-way point between the mid-stripe and the endline which is marked with a cone.

3. **2** takes it out of the air with one touch then with the second touch passes it to 3, then makes an accelerated run to **3**.

4. **3** receives ball from **2**, stops it with one touch, and accelerates on a bending run away from **3**'s position.

5. **2** arrives at stopped ball and serves a flighted ball to **3** who is now bending a run toward 1's original starting point.

6. The cycle continues in a circle for three minutes, then the direction of the runs is reversed for three minutes and you change your serving foot.

7. Players try to get as many serves in as possible (more serves equals more points.)

8. Players get points for successful serves (if <u>served</u> player can take serve out of the air on the run).

9. Serving feet are switched when direction of runs is switched. Right foot is used when rotating clockwise. Left foot is used when rotating counter-clockwise, although any direction will work with either foot.

10. Cones are placed halfway between the endline and the mid-stripe to force the players to serve past the cones, so their flighted balls have more distance.

Triangle Passing (midstripe to 18)

9/20/94			10/5/94			11/1/94			11/9/94			Cumulative		
Rank	Player	SP	Rank	Player	SP	Rank	Player	SP	Rank	Player	SP	Rank	Player	SP
1.	Wilson	11	1.	Santana	13	1.	Uritus	13	1.	Venturini	12	1.	Wilson	39
2.	Crow	10	2.	Egan	11	2.	Green	11	2.	Burns	11	2.	Santana	38
3.	Hutton	9	2.	Riggs	11	3.	Crow	10	2.	Santana	11	3.	Fettig	36
3.	Fettig	9	4.	Confer	10	4.	Santana	9	2.	Wilson	11	4.	Falk	35
5.	Johnson	8	4.	Falk	10	5.	Fettig	8	5.	Dacey	10	4.	Uritus	35
5.	Boyle	8	4.	Fettig	10	5.	Kelly	8	5.	Falk	10	6.	Burns	34
5.	Green	8	4.	Roberts	10	7.	Brooks	7	5.	Johnson	10	6.	Crow	34
5.	Byers	8	4.	Sanchez	10	7.	Burns	7	5.	Keller	10	6.	Venturini	34
5.	Falk	8	4.	Wilson	10	7.	Confer	7	5.	Kelly	10	9.	Green	32
10.	Dacey	7	10.	Brooks	9	7.	Falk	7	5.	Roberts	10	9.	Roberts	32
10.	Burns	7	10.	Burns	9	7.	Johnson	7	11.	Player 11	9	9.	Hutton	32
12.	Player 12	6	10.	Byers	9	7.	Keller	7	11.	Player 12	9	12.	Player 12	31
12.	Player 13	6	10.	Hutton	9	7.	Venturini	7	13.	Player 13	8	13.	Player 13	30
12.	Player 14	6	10.	Uritus	9	7.	Wilson	7	13.	Player 14	8	13.	Player 14	30
12.	Player 15	6	10.	Venturini	9	15.	Player 15	6	15.	Player 15	7	13.	Player 15	30
12.	Player 16	6	16.	Player 16	8	15.	Player 16	6	15.	Player 16	7	13.	Player 16	30
12.	Player 17	6	17.	Player 17	7	15.	Player 17	6	15.	Player 17	7	13.	Player 17	30
12.	Player 18	6	17.	Player 18	7	15.	Player 18	6	15.	Player 18	7	18.	Player 18	29
19.	Player 19	5	17.	Player 19	7	19.	Player 19	5	19.	Player 19	6	19.	Player 19	28
19.	Player 20	5	20.	Player 20	5	19.	Player 20	5	20.	Player 20	4	19.	Player 20	28
19.	Player 21	5	20.	Player 21	5	19.	Player 21	5	DNR	Boyle (6)		19.	Player 21	28
19.	Player 22	5	20.	Player 22	5	22.	Player 22	4		Hutton (8)		22.	Player 22	26
23.	Player 23	4	20.	Player 23	5	DNR	Byers (9)			Riggs (8)		23.	Player 23	23

SP = Successful Passes

The results are posted by week and cumulatively. DNR (did not run) players are given a number (in parentheses) based on their average up to that date. That way their cumulative total ranking is not adversely affected.

One v Ones to Goal •••••

One v Ones to Goal focuses the player on beating her opponent 1v1 on a full run to goal. This environment is not as psychologically taxing or as economical as the 1v1 to Cones, and you can see in the composite rankings, we don't give it as high a value (category multiplier). The drill was created to focus on running at people 1 v 1. It has a very game-impacting significance. The skills emphasized and developed in this drill win games.

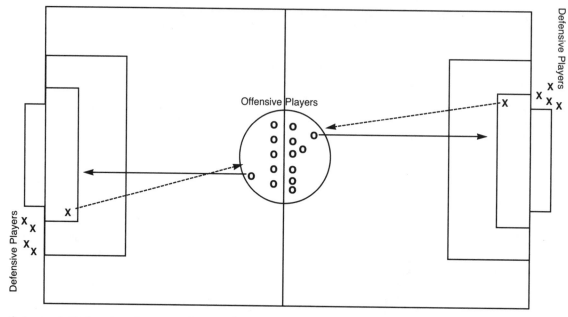

Set up: 1. Defensive players wait at endlines beside goals as in diagram.
2. Offensive players wait at the midstripe as in diagram.

Play: 1. Defensive player X serves long flighted ball (dashed line) to offensive player.
2. O dribbles ball toward goal (solid line) as X comes out to intercept her.
3. O tries to get to goal and score and X tries to stop O and clear the ball out to the mid stripe.
4. Runs can be made simultaneously at both ends of the field to speed things up.
5. Players get points based on their success:

offense (O): stuffed by X = 0 points
got shot off wide of goal = 1 point
got shot off on the face =2 points
beat X on dribble = 3 points
goal scored = 4 points

defense (X): stuffed = 4 points
let shot off wide = 3 points
let shot off on face = 2 points
beaten on dribble = 1 point
let goal in = 0 points

6. All offensive players go a set number of times (usually 4-5).
7. Defensive players rotate runs until offensive runs are finished, but try not to match up with the same attacker twice.
8. Midfielders are listed in both offensive and defensive categories and alternate runs. They are then scored in both categories that are posted.
9. Keepers can be scored and ranked as well.

134

One v Ones to Goal on 9/15

Offense Pos.		1	2	3	4	5	6	7	8			
Boyle	F	1	0	0	0					1/4	Stuffed by D	0
Burns	F	3	0	4	0					7/4	Got shot off: Wide	1
Confer	F	4	0	4	3					11/4	Got shot off: Face	2
Dacey	M	4	3	4	0					11/4	Beat D on Dribble	3
Egan	M	4	3	3	0					10/4	Scored Goal	4
Falk	F	3	4	2	4					13/4		
Green	F	0	2	0	1					3/4		
Johnson	F	0	0	0	3					3/4		
Keller	F	0	3	3	4					10/4		
Kelly	M	0	0	2	0					2/4		
Riggs	M	0	3	0	3					6/4		
Rubio	M	1	0	4	3					8/4		
Sanchez	M	1	2	0	1					4/4		
Uritus	M	2	3	1	0					6/4		
Venturini	M	0	0	3	4					7/4		
Defense												
Brooks	D	3	2	0	0					5/4	Scored on	0
Byers	D	0	1	1	4	0	0	1		7/7	Beaten on Dribble	1
Crow	D	2	4	1	4	4				15/5	Let shot off: Face	2
Dacey	M	2	1							3/2	Let shot off: Wide	3
Egan	M	0	3	1						4/3	Stuffed offense	4
Fettig	D	0	0	4	4	1	3			12/6		
Hutton	D	4	4	0	3	1	4			16/6		
Kelly	M	2	1							3/2		
Riggs	M	0	1							1/2		
Roberts	D	4	2	0	1	0				7/5		
Rubio	M	2	3	1						6/3		
Sanchez	M	4	1	4						9/3		
Santana	D	1	1	4	0	0	4			10/6		
Uritus	M	4	1	4	0					9/4		
Venturini	M	0	1	0						1/3		
Wilson	D	4	4	4	1	4				17/5		

   Points are awarded according to the key on the right. For example: Burns on offense beats Santana on defense on the dribble. Burns gets 3 points, Santana gets 1 point. All offensive players go a set number of times with defense stepping in as they please (hence the variety of the number of runs). Points per run are calculated at the left. For example: Dacey got 8 points in 4 runs, or 2 points per run.

   The person or people (if both ends of the field are used) that record this should do so as each run is made, scoring the offensive and defensive players. Standing at the mid-stripe with the players gives the best vantage point.

One v Ones to Goal • • • • •

1 v 1 to Goal Composite

8/30/94	9/15/94	
Offense	**Offense**	**Cumulative Offense**

8/30/94 Offense	9/15/94 Offense	Cumulative Offense
1. Venturini 2.50	1. Falk 3.25	1. Falk 3.25
2. Boyle 2.00	2. Confer 2.75	2. Confer 2.37
2. Confer 2.00	2. Dacey 2.75	2. Dacey 2.37
2. Dacey 2.00	4. Keller 2.50	4. Egan 2.25
2. Egan 2.00	4. Egan 2.50	5. Keller 2.12
6. Burns 1.75	6. Rubio 2.00	5. Venturini 2.12
6. Keller 1.75	7. Player 7 1.75	7. Player 7 1.75
6. Kelly 1.75	7. Player 8 1.75	7. Player 8 1.75
9. Player 9 1.50	9. Player 9 1.50	9. Player 9 1.50
9. Player 10 1.50	9. Player 10 1.50	9. Player 10 1.50
11. Player 11 1.00	11. Player 11 1.00	11. Player 11 1.12
12. Player 12 0.75	12. Player 12 0.75	11. Player 12 1.12
12. Player 13 0.75	12. Player 13 0.75	13. Player 13 1.00
Falk (injured)	14. Player 14 0.50	14. Player 14 0.75
Riggs (injured	15. Player 15 0.25	14. Player 15 0.75

8/30/94 Defense	9/15/94 Defense	Cumulative Defense
1. Sanchez 3.25	1. Wilson 3.40	1. Sanchez 3.12
2. Fettig 2.75	2. Crow 3.00	2. Crow 2.50
3. Uritus 2.60	2. Sanchez 3.00	3. Wilson 2.45
4. Santana 2.50	4. Hutton 2.75	4. Uritus 2.43
4. Byers 2.50	5. Uritus 2.25	5. Fettig 2.36
4. Wilson 2.50	6. Player 6 2.00	5. Hutton 2.36
7. Player 7 2.33	6. Player 7 2.00	7. Player 7 2.12
8. Player 8 2.25	8. Player 8 1.75	7. Player 8 2.12
9. Player 9 2.00	9. Player 9 1.50	9. Player 9 1.77
9. Player 10 2.00	9. Player 10 1.50	10. Player 10 1.75
11. Player 11 1.75	11. Player 11 1.40	11. Player 11 1.62
12. Player 12 1.50	12. Player 12 1.33	12. Player 12 1.45
13. Player 13 1.00	13. Player 13 1.25	13. Player 13 1.25
13. Player 14 1.00	14. Player 14 1.00	14. Player 14 1.16
15. Player 15 0.75	15. Player 15 0.50	15. Player 15 0.62
15. Player 16 0.75	16. Player 16 0.33	16. Player 16 0.54

Players are ranked based on the average points that they earn per run (or series). The single day is presented, and a cumulative average is kept (total points/total runs) and posted also. Players that did not participate are not ranked, such as Falk and Riggs on 8/30/94.

·····• Long Ball Service and Long Ball Heading

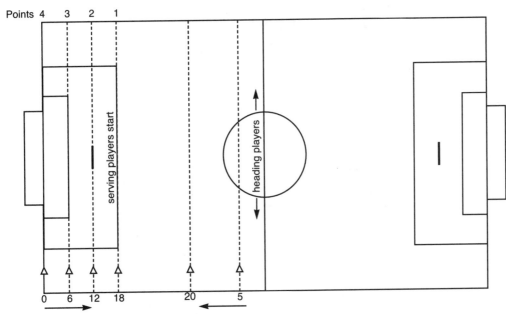

Set Up: 1. Cones are placed across the field at five and 20 yards from the mid-stripe and then at six, 12 and 18 yards from the endline.

2. Players are paired. One player lines up on the 18-yard line while the other lines up at the mid-stripe.

Play: 1. When the drill begins, players at the 18-yard line serve the ball to their partners near the mid-stripe with the right foot. The receiver then heads the ball back toward the server, trying to get it past the 20-yard mark.

2. If the server successfully serves the ball that distance, she moves back to the next line of cones (from the 18 to the 12) and serves with the right foot again. Her partner again tries to head it back past the 20-yard mark.

3. Every third serve is with the left foot, starting again at the 18. If the left-foot serve is successful, the server moves back a line the next time a left-footed serve comes around (every 3 serves). The server should alternate serves right, right, left, each time serving from the most successful position for each foot. (Left-footers use left, left, right rotation).

4. If the server fails to reach her partner with the serve, the next serve with that foot must be made from the previous line of cones. For it to count on the heading total and the serving total, the header has to be made within five yards of the mid-stripe. That's why the cones are there.

5. The server moves up or down the lines of cones, depending on the success or failure of the serve to reach the five-yard heading area.

6. The heading player keeps track of the number of successful heads past the 20-yard mark.

7. The server is awarded points for each foot according to the farthest positions served from with that foot. Points are indicated on the diagram above. The maximum number of combined points is eight.

8. The coach stops the drill after three minutes, and the partners switch positions and repeat the drill.

9. At the end of the drill, the players report their serving and heading scores to be recorded.

Long Serve/Heading on 11/21

Roster	Serve Position	# Of Headers
Bialas	2	3
Brallier	3	1
Confer	5	4
Dacey	3	3
Falk		
Fettig	5	3
Hutton	4	4
Johnson	4	3
Karvelsson		
Marslender	1	5
Keller	3	5
Parlow	3	7
Riggs	2	2
Roberts, A.	3	4
Roberts, T.	3	3
Rubio	3	2
Sheppard	3	4
Trojak	2	3
Uritus	4	6
Wilson	3	3

Serve position numbers and the number of headers are recorded on an alphabetical roster.

······ Long Ball Service and Long Ball Heading

Long Service
11/21/95

Long Serve Headers
11/21/95

			Cumulative			Cumulative		
Rank	Player	Serve Points	Rank	Player	Serve Points	Rank	Player	Serve Points
1.	Confer	6	1.	Confer	27	1.	Parlow	25
2.	Falk	4	2.	Falk	25	2.	Roberts, A.	24
2.	Karvelsson	4	3.	Fettig	24	3.	Uritus	22
2.	Uritus	4	4.	Karvelsson	20	4.	Confer	20
5.	Brallier	3	4.	Riggs	20	4.	Dacey	20
5.	Fettig	3	6.	Johnson	19	4.	Keller	20
5.	Hutton	3	7.	Keller	17	7.	Marslender	19
5.	Johnson	3	7.	Parlow	17	8.	Falk	17
5.	Riggs	3	7.	Uritus	17	8.	Fettig	17
5.	Roberts, T.	3	10.	Dacey	16	8.	Johnson	17
5.	Rubio	3	10.	Hutton	16	11.	Karvelsson	16
5.	Sheppard	3	10.	Rubio	16	12.	Player 12	15
13.	Player 13	2	13.	Player 13	15	12.	Player 13	15
13.	Player 14	2	13.	Player 14.	15	12.	Player 14	15
13.	Player 15	2	13.	Player 15.	15	15.	Player 15	14
13.	Player 16	2	13.	Player 16	15	15.	Player 16	14
13.	Player 17	2	17.	Player 17	13	16.	Player 17	13
18.	Player 18	1	17.	Player 18	13	18.	Player 18	12
18.	Player 19	1	19.	Player 19	12	19.	Player 19	10
18.	Player 20	1	20.	Player 20	6	20.	Player 20	8

The score for Long Serve Headers and Long Service is a cumulative number and is added to the cumulative total for the season to date. The players are then ranked by that total.

This composite was produced to provide an overall picture of a player's practice performance. We also do it to create intensity. Nobody wants to see their name on the bottom of the list. Still, it has given us other benefits. In our player conference that we hold three times a year, it gives us excellent objective material to review and motivate the players who are ambitious. Also, to a very good degree, it reflects their value as a competitive athlete on the field for us. There are exceptions, but not a large number. The area we still struggle with is objectively ranking heading, but we are still working on it. All of these ideas are a "work in progress" that we try to refine and improve every year as we learn more. Every drill for which statistics were kept was weighted and the final rankings for each organization were used.

Aerobic fitness, the ability to beat players one v one, speed and competitive ability were the most important factors in determining a player's value since these are considered to be the most important aspects of our game at the University of North Carolina. They were therefore given a 2X factor. One v Ones to Goal and Three Tier Shooting were the next most important evaluative statistics and so they were weighted with a 1X factor. Heading and Triangle passing were weighted with a 1/2X factor because the rankings did not fairly represent the skill levels of the players. Venturini, for example, was the best header on the team, but did not rank high on the heading ladder. And Fettig was the best passer/server and was only third in Triangle Passing.

Players names were set up on the chart as shown, and their rankings in each individual drill were entered. Then, based on the weight of the drill, the rank was either multiplied by two, one or one-half to give their rank a point value. The 1994, category multipliers also included a 2 1/2 and a three. All values for a player were then added across the chart to produce a total point value for each player. Since a higher ranking is indicated by a lower number, the players were ranked overall from the lowest total points to highest total points. For example: In 1994, Keller gets three points for the Cooper, half a point for 120s and half a point for Cones. She then received four points for anaerobic fitness, two points for her one v one skills, and four points for her One v One to Goal skills. Three Tier Shooting earned her five points, Heading 6.5 points, Triangle Passing 6.5 points, Speed 26 points and Most Competitive 8 points for a total of 66 points.

In the speed category, central players in the midfield and back (as noted by the asterisks) were given a category multiplier of 1X because their speed did not factor into their value as a player as much as it did in the other players. This is because the central positions did not require the speed the other positions did. Anaerobic fitness, which is surpassing aerobic fitness in importance among cutting-edge coaches, was factored into the composite, but not included in the pack because it is still an experimental statistic. We have not yet developed an effective way to evaluate the anaerobic data after the players have been tested. Consequently, the rankings could be considered unreliable, which is why they were only given a factor of 1X. That way, it affects the composite, but does not skew the overall rankings. I predict "anaerobic training" will be the new fitness buzz words for our game, and I hope the evolution of our matrix will reflect it properly.

1994 Final Statistical Composite Rankings •••••

Category	Aerobic Fitness			Anaerobic	1v1's	1v1's to Goal			3 T Shooting	Heading	Tri. Passing	Speed	M. Competitive	Total Pts.	Rank
Sub-Category	Cooper	120's	Cones			Off/Def	Offensive	Defensive							
Sub-Cat Multiplier	1X	1/2X	1/2X			1X	1/2X	1/2X							
Category Multiplier	2X			1X	2X	1X			1X	1/2X	1/2X	2X	2X		
Rank Player															
1. Keller, Debbie	3	1	1	4	1	4			5	13	13	13	4	66.0	1.
2. Sanchez, Keri	1	1	1	1	9		12	1	10	15	19	2	6	70.5	2.
3. Venturini, Tisha *	7	1	1	3	7		8	3	7	8	6	21	3	71.5	3.
4. Wilson, Staci	9	1	1	9	6	6			4	20	1	9	2	73.5	4.
5. Egan, Danielle	3	1	1	8	2		3	13	13	6	12	5	9	74.0	5.
6. Confer, Robin	12	5	10	2	4	10			3	1	19	8	12	92.5	6.
7. Santana, Rosalind	8	10	5	11	3	4			12	22	2	12	8	100.5	7.
8. Kelly, Angela	3	1	1	21	5		13	14	1	17	18	18	11	107.0	8.
9. Dacey, Sarah	11	15	1	12	14	6			2	9	13	14	5	116.0	9.
10. Roberts, Amy	3	1	1	5	10	11			16	14	9	7	18	117.5	10.
10. Uritus, Meg	12	5	5	17	10		1	2	6	4	4	17	9	117.5	10.
12. Player 12	2	1	1	10	10	9			15	22	6	10	14	119.0	12.
13. Player 13	16	15	2	15	10	2			7	12	4	6	20	128.5	13.
14. Player 14	17	10	15	14	19	5			22	3	6	22	1	137.0	14.
15. Player 15	12	15	10	23	14	7			16	18	3	15	7	138.0	15.
16. Player 16	17	10	20	16	20	5			11	10	22	1	18	158.0	16.
17. Player 17	21	15	1	19	16	9			7	5	9	16	15	165.0	17.
18. Player 18	22	20	5	13	8		11	12	14	16	13	23	16	181.5	18.
19. Player 19	20	15	1	7	18	15			23	11	9	20	12	183.0	19.
20. Player 20	12	15	5	18	17	8			18	22	13	11	22	183.5	20.
21. Player 21	17	20	5	20	22	7			20	21	23	4	17	184.5	21.
22. Player 22	23	10	1	22	21	10			21	7	19	3	23	188.5	22.
23. Player 23	10	15	1	6	23	14			19	2	13	19	21	190.5	23.
Rank Keeper															
1. Noonan, Tracy	2				1	1			4			2		13.0	1.
2. Finger, Shelly	3				2	2			1			3		16.0	2.
3. Keeper 3	3				4	3			2			1		18.0	3.
4. Keeper 4	1				3	4			3			4		22.0	4.

* Venturini's best quality: her extraordinary ability in the air is not reflected well in our system of ranking heading quality. We improved on it in 1995 by adding a very good category — "long serve heading." It was added to try to rectify Tisha's ridiculously low rank in this "objective" system. You can see where Venturini would have finished if she had finished "1" and we had strengthened the category like we did in 1995.

Category	Aerobic Fitness			Anaerobic	1v1's	1v1's to Goal			3T Shooting	Tri. Passing	Long Service	Heading		Speed	M. Competitive		
Sub-Category	Cooper	120's	Cones			Off/Def	Offensive	Defensive				Long Serve	Ladder				
Sub-Cat Multiplier	1X	1/2X	1/2X			1X	1/2X	1/2X				1/2X	1/2X				
Category Multiplier		2X		1X	3X	1X	1X		1X	1/2X	1/2X	1X		2X	2 1/2X	Total Pts.	Rank
Rank Player																	
1. Parlow, Cindy	3	2	1	19	5		3	7	13	1	8	1	1	5	1	74.5	1.
2. Keller, Debbie (1)	5	1	2	8	5	5			3	5	7	6	10	11	3	81.0	2.
3. Confer, Robin (6)	18	1	10	9	2	1			13	8	1	6	6	3	5	81.5	3.
4. Wilson, Staci (4)	10	1	10	9	1	1			10	3	16	13	16	8	7	96.0	4.
5. Falk, Aubrey (13)	11	1	10	15	4		6	7	1	8	3	8	8	1	12	96.5	5.
6. Karvelsson, Rakel	1	1	10	9	10		2	2	16	10	4	10	5	9	2	101.0	6.
7. Roberts, Tiffany	4	1	1	1	3		4	6	19	14	11	19	12	2	13	103.5	7.
8. Fettig, Nel (15)	8	3	10	5	8	3			5	1	2	8	20	15	9	104.5	8.
9. Uritus, Meg (10)	15	3	4	20	7		8	5	4	15	8	3	2	13	4	107.0	9.
10. Roberts, Amy (10)	7	1	1	3	9	13			2	10	8	2	11	6	16	120.5	10.
11. Rubio, Vanessa	20	4	10	9	12		9	9	6	10	14	17	14	4	6	137.5	11.
12. Player 12	16	5	9	17	11		10	14	8	7	11	4	9	12	8	146.5	12.
13. Player 13	6	1	10	6	15		7	10	7	10	17	13	19	16	11	151.0	13.
14. Player 14	9	1	10	4	14	17			15	18	14	20	13	7	10	164.0	14.
15. Player 15	1	1	1	18	18	12			12	4	6	10	4	10	14	165.0	15.
16. Player 16	17	15	10	16	13	11			20	16	11	13	3	17	19	201.5	16.
17. Player 17	14	3	5	2	17	15			18	17	17	12	7	14	18	203.5	16.
18. Player 18	19	15	10	9	16		11	4	9	5	5	18	18	20	15	205.5	18.
19. Player 19	11	1	6	6	19		13	12	11	19	20	4	15	18	20	216.0	19.
20. Player 20	11	11	3	9	20		14	16	17	20	19	16	17	19	17	235.5	20.
Rank Keeper																	
1. Noonan, Tracy (1)	1			1					1					3		12.5	1.
2. Mullinix, Siri	3			2					2					1		13.5	2.
3. Keeper 3	2			4					4					2		23.0	3.
4. Keeper 4	4			3					3					4		26.0	4.

Notes: Final rankings for each category are indicated in boxes (1 to 20)
Ranking is multiplied by multiplier (importance of category)
All categories' multiplied scores are added for total
Central players (Uritus, Sheppard, Fettig, Hutton) have multiplier of 1X; Dacey has 1.5X in speed because it is not as critical in the center of midfield or at sweeper.
In the parentheses after the names of the upperclassmen is the previous year's rank. Rubio improved the most in one season going from 21st in 1994 to 11th in 1995. Her contribution on the field reflected this huge improvement.

Chapter 17

Computer Analysis

"I genuinely feel this is the beginning of the second revolution in match analysis, the first being videotape."

During the 1995 NSCAA Convention, I sat down in the back of Zvi Friedman's computer analysis lecture. I sat down to get organized and see what clinic I had underlined to attend next, and purely by accident, I got involved in watching Zvi's session. Personally, I have always felt I was born into the wrong century — even a typewriter is beyond my technological grasp. I organize myself on legal pads, and part of my comfort in seeing Tony DiCicco succeed me as national team coach was his expertise on a computer. I knew he could take us into the next century.

Zvi was doing the session with Bora Milutinovic, and they were showing us how this software could break down opponents, analyze his own team's performance, statistically categorize individual performances ... it seemed to be able to do anything. I was very impressed. At the end of the session, I walked up to Zvi and told him very quickly how wonderful I thought his software was because it broke down a game so objectively. It did for games what we try to do in practice — make every player accountable for performance. But since it involved a computer, never in my wildest imagination did I feel I would be able to use it. So I left to see the next session.

Zvi hunted me down during that convention. He left the software at the hotel desk for me (which I never picked up, by the way) and began calling me each month to see if I wanted to try it during my college season. Frankly, I never really knew how simple the entire process was. Through unbelievable luck, I was doing a camp in Southern California that spring, and he wanted to show me some things about the software during our lunch break. So while I was eating a tuna sub, he showed me the entire process of how simple the data was assembled, and I could not believe it. It finally struck me that even I could do this, and it finally struck Zvi that I had no idea it was so simple. Now I understood and I wanted it for my 1995 college season. I felt with the serious graduation losses we were about to endure, we would need every edge possible to stay competitive. The software produced so much detail and had so many possibilities, I also wanted Zvi and his partner, Jon Kotas, to help me analyze the 1995 Women's World Championship in Sweden for FIFA's Technical Study Group. Following the world championship, even FIFA was impressed and printed an article about it in one of their publications.

Obviously, now I am sold on his product. I genuinely feel it is the beginning of the second revolution in match analysis, the first being videotape. It also gives you a different view of the game, categorizing successes and failures numerically and showing patterns graphically. I think if used in conjunction with videotape, it gives a more complete analysis. I also feel this has a particular impact on the development of the female athlete, since it is clear there is no personal criticism in this kind of statistical review. This objective form of criticism makes the point without undermining rapport and support between player and coach, which with many young athletes is important for confidence.

Given the hectic game-dense college season, this system of analysis gives you a faster and more distilled view than video. I am just starting to see all the different ways we can use this effectively. But even this first season, we kept an individual player's match performance in a binder for anyone to see in our team meeting room. We have a page on each player's performance, assessing number of balls won, lost, received, successful passes made, possessional percentage, impact passes (how many of their passes ultimately resulted in a shot on goal), player range (you will see Robin Confer's player range on Page 148), pass distribution (who received the most passes), the spine (we have reproduced six game spines for you) and the traditional goals, assists and shots. Next season, we will have a new bulletin board with match performance rankings just like the bulletin board we have for practice performance. What follows in the book is just a small part of what we pulled off the software for our own use. And it's real value is if it can give us a performance accountability that we can be challenged to improve upon the next time we play.

I hope you find it interesting.

1995 UNC WOMEN'S SOCCER

Computer Match Analysis · Game Performance Comparison

Obviously, when you play an opponent twice in the same season, you want to challenge your team to improve between matches. Unquestionably, you are at a motivational disadvantage if you won the first matchup, but your challenge remains nonetheless. Here are three outstanding opponents and the computer comparison of how we played the two games against them in 1995.

VS. DUKE

Category	First Game	Second Game	Change in UNC Performance
UNC Goals Scored	4	4	0%
UNC Shots Taken	24	24	0%
UNC Passes Made	535	552	plus 3%
UNC Complete Pass %	53.6	46.1	minus 14%
Pass Interceptions by UNC	224	294	plus 31%
Shots by Opponent	5	2	plus 60%
Goals by Opponent	1	0	plus

VS. SANTA CLARA

Category	First Game	Second Game	Change in UNC Performance
UNC Goals Scored	2	2	0%
UNC Shots Taken	17	24	plus 41%
UNC Passes Made	308	451	plus 46%
UNC Complete Pass %	49.6	50	0%
Pass Interceptions by UNC	140	229	plus 64%
Shots by Opponent	8	5	plus 38%
Goals by Opponent	0	0	0%

VS. NOTRE DAME

Category	First Game	Second Game	Change in UNC Performance
UNC Goals Scored	2	0	minus
UNC Shots Taken	33	30	minus 9%
UNC Passes Made	492	483	minus 1%
UNC Complete Pass %	57.1	52.5	minus 8%
Pass Interceptions by UNC	213	193	minus 8%
Shots by Opponent	10	8	plus 20%
Goals by Opponent	0	1	minus

UNC GOALS – SCORED

Rank	Opponent	Goals Scored
1.	Notre Dame – NCAA Semifinal	0
3.	Notre Dame	2
3.	Santa Clara	2
3.	Santa Clara – NCAA Regional	2
13.	Duke	4
13.	Duke – ACC Semifinal	4

OPPONENT GOALS SCORED

Rank	Opponent	Goals
1.	Notre Dame – NCAA Semifinal	1
1.	Duke	1
6.	Notre Dame	0
6.	Santa Clara	0
6.	Santa Clara – NCAA Regional	0
6.	Duke – ACC Semifinal	0

UNC SHOTS – TAKEN

Rank	Opponent	Shots
2.	Santa Clara	17
6.	Santa Clara – NCAA Regional	24
6.	Duke	24
6.	Duke – ACC Semifinal	24
14.	Notre Dame – NCAA Semifinal	30
15.	Notre Dame	33

SHOTS BY OPPONENT

Rank	Opponent	Shots
1.	Notre Dame	10
2.	Santa Clara	8
2.	Notre Dame – NCAA Semifinal	8
11.	Santa Clara – NCAA Regional	5
11.	Duke	5
18.	Duke – ACC Semifinal	2

UNC PASSES MADE

Rank	Opponent	# Passes
1.	Santa Clara	308
3.	Santa Clara – NCAA Regional	451
9.	Notre Dame – NCAA Semifinal	483
11.	Notre Dame	492
20.	Duke	535
22.	Duke – ACC Semifinal	552

UNC COMPLETE PASS %

Rank	Opponent	Completion %
1.	Duke – ACC Semifinal	46.1
2.	Santa Clara	49.6
5.	Santa Clara – NCAA Regional	50.0
9.	Notre Dame – NCAA Semifinal	52.5
10.	Duke	53.6
16.	Notre Dame	57.1

PASS INTERCEPTIONS BY UNC

Rank	Opponent	Pass Intcpt
2.	Santa Clara	140
7.	Notre Dame – NCAA Semifinal	193
15.	Notre Dame	213
18.	Duke	224
19.	Santa Clara – NCAA Regional	229
24.	Duke – ACC Semifinal	294

1995 UNC WOMEN'S SOCCER

Computer Match Analysis • <u>Passing Standards by Position for NCAA Play</u>

VANDERBILT – NCAA REG

		Balls Won	Balls Lost	W/L Ratio	Total Receptions	%Recept Lost
Forwards	Keller	16	31	.5/1	60	52
	Confer	7	23	.33/1	40	58
	Parlow	20	21	1.00/1	53	40
	Average	14	25	1.00/2	51	50
Midfield	Dacey	7	13	.5/1	23	56
	Sheppard	19	16	1.2/1	43	37
	T. Roberts	21	16	1.3/1	38	42
	Uritus	15	9	1.66/1	33	27
	Average	16	14	1.00/1	34	41
Backs	Fettig	22	22	1.00/1	54	41
	A. Roberts	21	12	1.75/1	33	36
	Wilson	33	21	1.6/1	48	43
	Average	25	55	1.00/2	45	40

	Impact Passes	Shots
Parlow	13	6
Confer	10	7
T. Roberts	8	4
Keller	8	7
Sheppard	6	2
Uritus	5	2
Fettig	2	3
Wilson	1	3
Dacey	1	0

SANTA CLARA – NCAA QUARTER

		Balls Won	Balls Lost	W/L Ratio	Total Receptions	%Recept Lost
Forwards	Keller	10	27	.40/1	42	64
	Confer	7	23	.30/1	43	53
	Parlow	19	24	.80/1	52	46
	Average	12	25	1.00/2	46	54
Midfield	Dacey	17	11	1.5/1	38	28
	Sheppard	5	8	.63/1	16	50
	T. Roberts	14	16	.90/1	36	44
	Uritus	21	14	1.33/1	37	38
	Average	15	12	1.25/1	32	40
Backs	Fettig	40	36	1.11/1	59	61
	A. Roberts	16	15	1.00/1	28	54
	Wilson	34	25	1.36/1	39	64
	Average	30	25	1.25/1	42	60

	Impact Passes	Shots
Parlow	7	3
Confer	6	7
Keller	5	3
Dacey	4	2
Wilson	3	1
Sheppard	1	2
Uritus	1	1
Fettig	1	3

NOTRE DAME – NCAA SEMI

		Balls Won	Balls Lost	W/L Ratio	Total Receptions	%Recept Lost
Forwards	Keller	7	26	.27/1	43	61
	Confer	13	15	.90/1	32	46
	Parlow	16	22	.75/1	54	29
	Average	12	21	1.00/2	43	45
Midfield	Dacey	12	6	1.5/1	24	25
	Sheppard	5	5	1.00/1	8	62
	T. Roberts	15	13	1.2/1	32	41
	Uritus	14	17	.82/1	31	55
	Average	12	10	1.25/1	23	46
Backs	Fettig	28	26	1.1/1	48	54
	A. Roberts	21	8	2.6/1	27	29
	Wilson	21	14	1.5/1	31	45
	Average	23	16	1.5/1	35	43

	Impact Passes	Shots
Confer	5	4
Wilson	4	1
Parlow	3	7
Uritus	3	1
Fettig	3	1
Keller	2	5
Dacey	1	1

With time, we will be able to see the evolution of our team and players over the course of their NCAA careers. The statistics will certainly reflect the level of our opponent and the level of that year's team. Also as the software improves, this soccer "boxscore" will be able to provide more telling information for the players, coaches, media and fans.

Impact passes are all passes in the possessional sequence that contribute to a shot being made — in effect, assists on shots. An impact pass is not just the last pass before a shot, but any one of the passes in the unbroken sequence (after you win possession) that result in a shot.

1995 UNC WOMEN'S SOCCER
Computer Match Analysis
Opponents Ranked by Category

Some columns are skewed for different reasons: UNC SHOTS TAKEN and SHOTS BY OPPONENT have greater shot totals than the official scorer, but the computer does not subjectively eliminate any shot. PASS INTERCEPTIONS BY UNC is certainly affected by how well we possess the ball. In some games, we possessed the ball at will and had fewer chances to intercept as a result.

Teams are ranked according to performance. The better a team performed against UNC, the higher it is ranked in each category.

Data for the following games was interpolated from the available data on the game: Duke – ACC Semifinals • Florida International Indiana • Maryland (regular season) N.C. State (regular season) • San Francisco

Data for the following games was not available by computer because of existing weather conditions at game time: Florida State (regular season) – Monsoon rains Stanford – Lack of shade (couldn't see laptop screen)

UNC GOALS – SCORED

Rank Opponent	Goals Scored
1. Notre Dame – NCAA Semi	0
2. Clemson	1
3. Florida	2
3. Notre Dame	2
3. Santa Clara	2
3. Santa Clara – NCAA Reg	2
3. St. Mary's	2
8. Maryland – ACC Final	3
8. Virginia	3
8. Wake Forest	3
8. Maryland	3
8. Wisconsin-Madison	3
13. Team 13	4
13. Team 14	4
13. Team 15	4
16. Team 16	5
17. Team 17	6
17. Team 18	6
17. Team 19	6
20. Team 20	7
21. Team 21	8
21. Team 22	8
23. Team 23	9
23. Team 24	9

UNC SHOTS – TAKEN

Rank Opponent	Shots
1. Maryland – ACC Final	13
2. Santa Clara	17
3. Florida	18
4. Virginia	22
5. Maryland	23
6. Duke	24
6. Santa Clara – NCAA Reg	24
6. William & Mary	24
6. Duke – ACC Semi	24
10. St. Mary's	28
11. Clemson	29
11. Wisconsin – Madison	29
11. Wisconsin – Milwaukee	29
14. Team 14	30
15. Team 15	33
15. Team 16	33
17. Team 17	34
17. Team 18	34
19. Team 19	36
20. Team 20	37
21. Team 21	39
22. Team 22	41
23. Team 23	48
24. Team 24	49

UNC PASSES MADE

Rank Opponent	# Passes
1. Santa Clara	308
2. Wisconsin-Madison	407
3. Santa Clara – NCAA Reg	451
3. William & Mary	451
5. Clemson	459
6. Maryland – ACC Final	464
7. Wisconsin-Milwaukee	468
8. Florida	476
9. Notre Dame – NCAA Semi	483
10. St. Mary's	487
11. Notre Dame	492
12. Virginia	504
12. Maryland	504
14. Team 14l	508
15. Team 15	517
16. Team 16	519
17. Team 17	521
18. Team 18	522
19. Team 19	526
20. Team 20	535
21. Team 21	545
22. Team 22	552
23. Team 23	574
24. Team 24	632

PASS INTERCEPTIONS BY UNC

Rank Opponent	Pass Intcpt
1. Wisconsin-Milwaukee	119
2. Santa Clara	140
3. Colorado College	165
4. Florida International	166
5. Indiana	184
6. Wisconsin-Madison	185
7. Notre Dame – NCAA Semi	193
8. William & Mary	199
9. Radford	201
10. Wake Forest	203
11. San Francisco	208
11. NC State	208
13. Team 13	212
13. Team 14	212
15. Team 15	213
16. Team 16	216
17. Team 17	219
18. Team 18	224
19. Team 19	229
20. Team 20	233
21. Team 21	238
22. Team 22	254
23. Team 23	263
24. Team 24	294

OPPONENT GOALS SCORED

Rank Opponent	Goals Scored
1. Colorado College	1
1. Duke	1
1. Notre Dame – NCAA Semi	1
1. William & Mary	1
1. Wisconsin-Madison	1
6. Clemson	0
6. Duke – ACC Semi	0
6. Fla. St. –ACC 1st Rnd	0
6. Florida	0
6. Florida International	0
6. Indiana	0
6. Maryland	0
6. Maryland – ACC Final	0
6. NC State	0
6. Notre Dame	0
6. Radford	0
6. San Francisco	0
6. Santa Clara	0
6. Santa Clara – NCAA Reg	0
6. St. Mary's	0
6. Vanderbilt – NCAA Reg	0
6. Virginia	0
6. Wake Forest	0
6. Wisconsin-Milwaukee	0

SHOTS BY OPPONENT

Rank Opponent	Shots
1. Notre Dame	10
2. Santa Clara	8
2. William & Mary	8
2. Notre Dame – NCAA Semi	8
5. Florida	7
5. St. Mary's	7
5. Vanderbilt – NCAA Reg	7
5. Wisconsin-Madison	7
9. Maryland – ACC Final	6
9. Maryland	6
11. Duke	5
11. Santa Clara – NCAA Reg	5
13. Team 13	4
13. Team 14	4
13. Team 15	4
16. Team 16	3
16. Team 17	3
18. Team 18	2
19 Team 19	1
19. Team 20	1
19. Team 21	1
19. Team 22	1
19. Team 23	1
24. Team 24	0

UNC COMPLETE PASS %

Rank Opponent	Completion %
1. Duke – ACC Semi	46.1
2. Santa Clara	49.6
3. Maryland – ACC Final	49.7
4. Maryland	49.9
5. Santa Clara – NCAA Reg	50.0
6. Florida	50.1
7. Virginia	50.9
8. Clemson	51.3
9. Notre Dame – NCAA Semi	52.5
10. Duke	53.6
11. Wisconsin-Madison	54.2
12. San Francisco	55.0
13 Team 13	55.7
14. Team 14	55.9
15. Team 15	56.6
16. Team 16	57.1
17. Team 17	57.8
18. Team 18	58.5
19. Team 19	60.5
20. Team 20	62.5
21. Team 21	63.8
22. Team 22	67.2
23. Team 23	68.2
24. Team 24	72.3

1995 UNC WOMEN'S SOCCER
Computer Match Analysis Opponents Rankings

RANKING FOR EACH INDIVIDUAL STATISTIC

Overall Rank Opponent	UNC Goals Scored	UNC Shots Taken	UNC Passes Made	UNC Compl Pass%	Pass Intercept By UNC	Shots by Opponent	Goals by Opponent	Ave. Rank
1. Santa Clara	3	2	1	2	2	2	6	2.57
2. Notre Dame – NCAA Sem	1	14	9	9	7	2	1	6.14
3. Florida	3	3	8	6	13	5	6	6.29
3. Wisconsin-Madison	8	11	2	11	6	5	1	6.29
5. Santa Clara – NCAA Reg	3	6	3	5	19	11	6	7.57
5. Maryland – ACC Final	8	1	6	3	20	9	6	7.57
7. William & Mary	16	6	3	19	8	2	1	7.86
8. Clemson	2	11	5	8	16	13	6	8.71
9. St. Mary's	3	10	10	15	13	5	6	8.86
10. Notre Dame	3	15	11	16	15	1	6	9.57
10. Maryland	8	5	12	4	23	9	6	9.57
12. Wisconsin-Milwaukee	2	11	7	22	1	19	6	9.71
13. Team 13	8	6	20	10	18	11	1	10.57
14. Team 14	8	4	12	7	22	16	6	10.71
15. Team 15	14	20	16	13	17	5	6	13.00
15. Team 16	14	6	22	1	24	18	6	13.00
17. Team 17	20	21	17	17	3	13	1	13.14
18. Team 18	17	17	19	12	11	16	6	14.00
19. Team 19	8	15	21	20	10	19	6	14.14
20. Team 20	17	19	14	21	4	19	6	14.29
20. Team 21	17	17	18	18	5	19	6	14.29
22. Team 22	21	22	15	14	11	24	6	16.14
23. Team 23	23	24	23	23	9	19	6	18.14
24. Team 24	23	23	24	24	21	13	6	19.14

Don't be confused by a direct reading of the columns. These are rankings of opponents' success against all the games we played in 1995. So reading across the Santa Clara column, "UNC Goals Scored" was not 3 goals, but Santa Clara was third best in the category with two goals, tied with Florida, St. Mary's, Notre Dame and Santa Clara in the NCAA Tournament; "UNC Shots Taken" was not 2 shots, but Santa Clara held us to the second-lowest number of shots (17) of all our opponents. For the number of goals, shots, passes made, and all other stats, see page 144.

UNC vs. Santa Clara – September 29, 1995

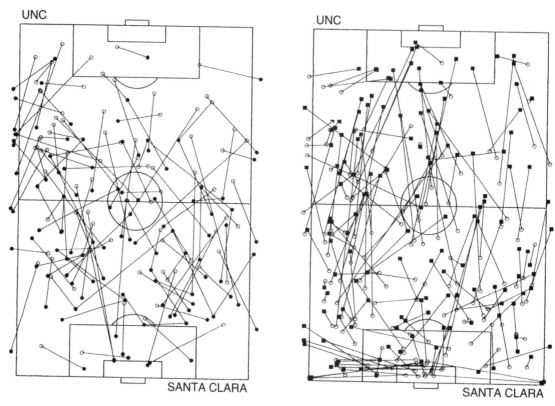

This graphic shows completed passes
by Santa Clara

This graphic shows passes lost by UNC

In between the two Santa Clara games, we sat down with several players and showed them the computer information when we thought it would contribute to a better performance. We thought Sarah Dacey could play better if we just showed her the graphics of her first performance.

She was our right midfielder in our first game with Santa Clara, so since we are attacking the goal at the bottom of the page, she would be on the left side. We showed her how many passes Santa Clara was completing in her zone, relative to the zone dominated by Tiffany Roberts on the opposite side (left midfielder). We showed Sarah how many balls were given away in her zone relative to any other midfield zone on the field.

Sarah certainly took the criticism positively because her second game against

Santa Clara was outstanding. Here are her statistical comparisons of the two games:

Date	Balls Won	Balls Lost	Total Receptions	%Reception Lost
9/25/95	7	10	24	42%
11/25/95	17	11	37	29%

The "passes given away" stat for the second game is misleading. In the second game, she had a much greater number of possessions. This, however, is reflected in the much-improved "percentage receptions lost" stat. This comparison is not as pure as we would like since for much of the second game against Santa Clara we played Sarah in the center, but her performance in the second game was a radical improvement, and I'm sure the objective review of the computer helped her to see that she could do much more.

Flooding Zones

Flooding zones is a term we use to describe patterns of runs up top when we are attacking through our flank midfielders. When you flood zones, your strikers are all "flooding" over onto one side of the field to create numbers around the anticipated service zones. It also clears the opposite side of the field if the defense tracks the striker. It's designed to pull defenses apart. Flooding zones requires a lot of energy from the players. Flooding zones offensively all the time places very high demands on the players. The best prospect of service into a flooded attacking zone is when the ball is on the flank in midfield. You want all the strikers within service distance of that ball. The choreographic pattern if the ball is at the feet of your left midfielder is to have the left wing check short up the line or short into the center if you want to clear a flank channel for the center forward. The center forward has two options: To run on a diagonal down the flank or show in the center. These options are based on the runs of the left wing in front of her, and the time the server has on the ball. More time permits a deeper run to the flank; less time dictates an earlier check in the center. The left wing has one simple but exhausting option: sprint right at the opponent's sweeper and make sure she is not able to get anything that skips through.

The graphics beginning on the next page show Robin Confer's mobility and range during the 1995 season. Since flooding zones is a sideline-to-sideline demand, it's critical that our front-runners cover a lot of ground. For us to effectively flood zones, Robin should be receiving the ball at a variety of points around the field. We also want our front-runners to track their marks back into the midfield and into the defensive third as well. Each dot on the graphic represents a place where Robin touched the ball. You can see how hard she works and how much she improved as the season wore on.

UNC vs. Wake Forest – September 26, 1995

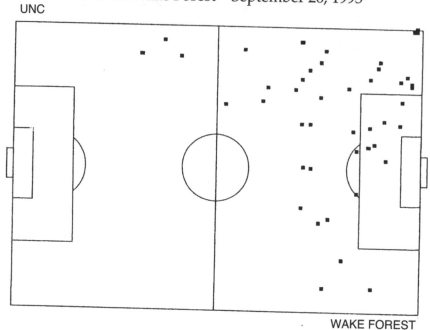

UNC vs. Duke – October 19, 1995

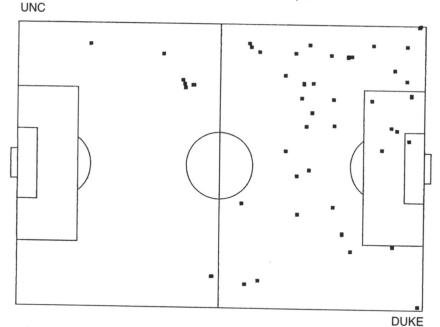

These four graphics show the positive progression of Robin Confer's player range during the 1995 season. In our attacking system of "flooding zones" you want to see your strikers all over the field up top. This demonstrates high mobility. You also want to see them tracking back to double up with your midfield or to follow their marks as they penetrate. You can see Robin's steady improvement as she started to cover more and more ground — offensively and defensively — as the season progressed. Each dot is where Robin touched the ball.

UNC vs. Maryland – November 5, 1995

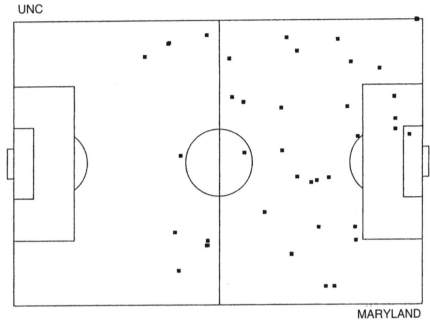

UNC vs. Notre Dame – December 1, 1995

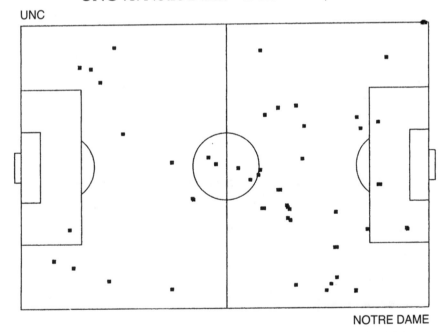

The efficiency of this assessment of "mobility" versus the time-consuming videotape review is apparent. Also the clear picture that this gives is a wonderful teaching tool for the player who with one glance can see an entire game's mobility. This will eventually capture the cliché "paint the field."

The Spine

The "Spine" gives you a very graphic look at how your players connect with each other during the game. Obviously, you would love to see thick lines all over the field because it demonstrates a wonderful possessional inter-passing through your unit. Your opponent's pressure and your own capacity to hold the ball will dictate how thick your lines are. This also illustrates who "shows" well for the ball, who likes to pass to whom and the directional flow of your attack.

Don't be deceived by the static positioning of the ten field players. The distribution and placement of the players is spaced as much as possible. They are placed in the general shape of where they are positioned when the game begins. You can also see us adjust based on the shape of our opponents. Duke and Santa Clara attacked generally with two front-runners, so you can see us match up with three in the back, four in the midfield and three up front. Against Notre Dame, we had to play with an extra defender (Rubio), drop out a midfielder (Sheppard) and play with four in the back, three in the midfield and three up front.

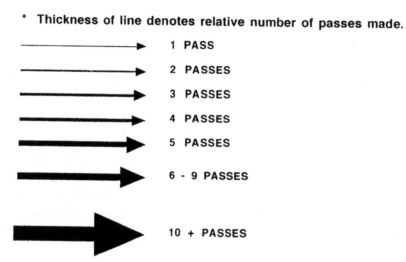

* **Thickness of line denotes relative number of passes made.**

1 PASS

2 PASSES

3 PASSES

4 PASSES

5 PASSES

6 - 9 PASSES

10 + PASSES

UNC SPINE vs.SANTA CLARA 9-29-95

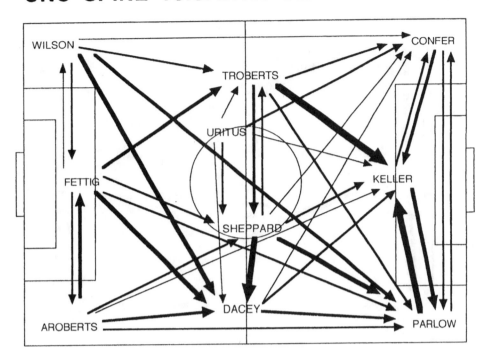

UNC SPINE vs. SANTA CLARA 11-25-95

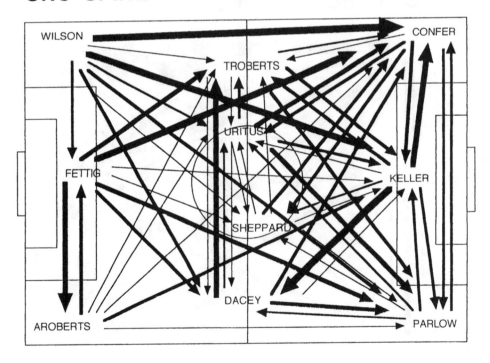

UNC SPINE vs. DUKE 10-19-95

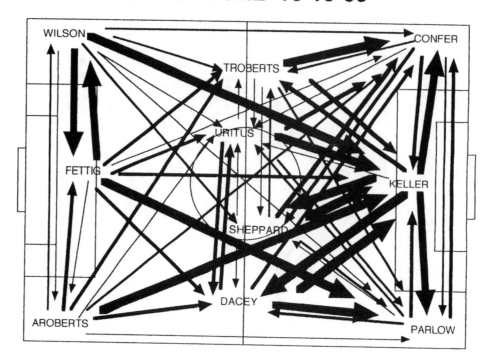

UNC SPINE vs. DUKE 11-3-95

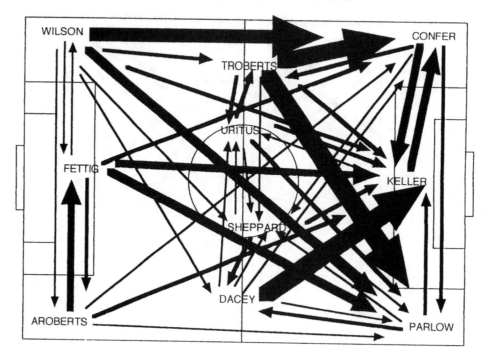

UNC SPINE vs. NOTRE DAME 10-15-95

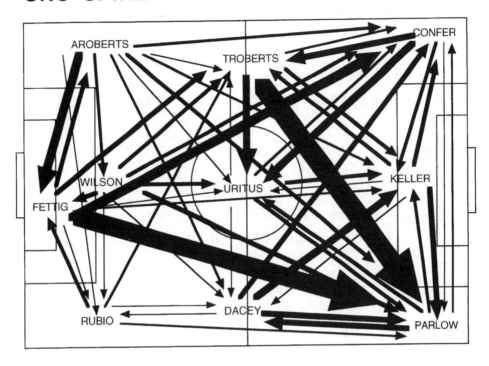

UNC SPINE vs. NOTRE DAME 12-1-95

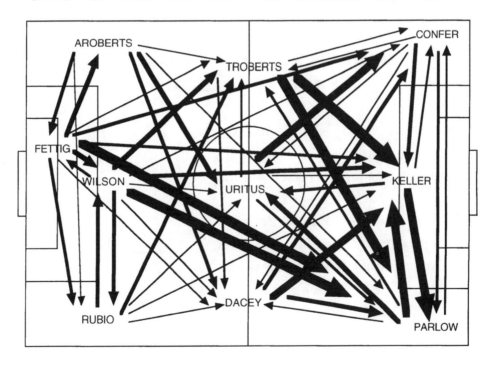

Recommended Reading List

Understanding Gender Difference

- **In a Different Voice — Carol Gilligan**
  Men and women think differently
- **You Just Don't Understand — Deborah Tannen**
  Men and women speak differently
- **The Female Advantage — Sally Helgesen**
  Men and women lead and are led differently
- **The Difference — Judy Mann**
  Boys and girls are raised differently
- **Men are from Mars, Women are from Venus — John Gray**
  Men and women relate to each other differently
- **Sappho Was a Right-On Woman — Sidney Abbott and Barbara Love**
  Understanding lesbianism

Developing Your People, Your Leaders and Your Team

- **The Road Less Traveled — M. Scott Peck**
  Developing people
- **On Becoming A Leader — Warren Bennis**
  Developing leaders
- **The Different Drum — M. Scott Peck**
  Developing "community" in your team
- **Greater Expectations — William Damon**
  Expecting more from your people, leaders and teams

Developing Your Game

- **They Call Me Coach — John Wooden**
  Being a role model
- **The Winner Within — Pat Riley**
  Coaching considerations beyond the practice arena
- **Soccer Coaching The Modern Way — Eric Batty**
  A simple view of our game in 1968
- **Soccer Tactics and skills — Charles Hughes**
  A more detailed view of our game in 1980
- **Soccer Coaching: The European Way — Edited by Eric Batty**
  A collection of excellent ideas from outstanding coaches
- **Soccer Fundamentals for Players and Coaches — Weil Coerver**
  Teaching soccer players how to move with the ball, fundamental 1v1
- **United States Soccer Football Association Coaches Manual — Detmar Cramer**
  Still one of the most complete overviews I have ever seen.
- **National Soccer Coaches Association of America National and Advanced National Coaching Curriculum — Jim Lennox**
  Thorough, detailed and well-organized approach to coaching our game.